NATIONAL PARKS

OF NEW ZEALAND

Jimbo

Hope the beauty of New Zealand will touch your heart and lift your spirits......

with Love

Ruki

NATIONAL PARKS
OF NEW ZEALAND

CRAIG POTTON

CRAIG
POTTON
PUBLISHING

Photography: Craig Potton
Text: Annie Wheeler
Additional writing: David Chowdhury
Maps: One Sky Design
Design, layout and production: Robbie Burton & Tina Delceg
Filmwork: Astra Print Ltd, Wellington
Printed by Everbest Printing Ltd, Hong Kong

ISBN 0 908802 42 0 (softcover)
ISBN 0 908802 48 X (hardcover)

First Published in 1998

CONTENTS

INTRODUCTION

The practise of wilderness preservation was still in its infancy when the summits of the sacred Central North Island volcanoes Tongariro and Ruapehu were offered to the nation as a national park in 1887. Tongariro National Park, as it became known, was New Zealand's first and only the fourth national park in the world, its formation made possible by the vision of Tuwharetoa paramount chief Te Heuheu Tukino IV, and the tireless work of the artist, politician and preservationist William Fox.

Since 1887, 12 more national parks covering over 10 per cent of New Zealand have been created, guaranteeing absolute protection for all landforms, plants and animals within their boundaries. In 110 years New Zealand's national parks network has been developed to include an astonishing variety of wild landscapes – from the unpredictable volcanic highlands of Tongariro and the mystical forests and lakes of Te Urewera, to the lowland forests, rugged glaciated mountains and wild coastlines of Westland and Fiordland.

The international significance of the distinctive flora and fauna that inhabit these diverse landscapes – relic survivors of ancient Gondwanaland which have evolved in isolation from other land for between 60–80 million years – has long been acknowledged by science. However, the early legislation that governed national parks determined they would be created largely for their scenic grandeur, not for their ecological value. This, combined

Above: A tree fern is framed by two enormous beech trunks near Lake Waikareiti in Te Urewera National Park.

Opposite: Sweeping ridges and summits above valleys with high, near vertical, walls typify the grandeur of Fiordland National Park. This aerial view was taken above the Arthur valley looking north towards the peaks of Mount Aspiring National Park on the distant skyline.

with a desire to utilise all potential agricultural lands, meant the first national parks had a distinct bias towards 'unproductive' mountain areas, while ecologically important lowland forests and other natural areas that lacked the visual qualities of mountain ranges were overlooked.

Change took place when the National Parks Act was amended in 1980 to allow places of high ecological value (these were often sites also under threats from logging and/or mining) to be considered for national park status. This new emphasis allowed the addition in 1982 of the large ecologically rich lowland forests of South Okarito and Waikukupa to Westland National Park, and the creation of the Paparoa and Kahurangi National Parks in 1987 and 1996 respectively.

New Zealand's outstanding natural treasures have been recognised by UNESCO several times, for example with the granting of dual world heritage status (for its natural features and cultural importance) to Tongariro National Park, and the creation in 1990 of the vast Te Wahipounamu South-West New Zealand World Heritage Area, which incorporates Westland, Mount Cook, Mount Aspiring and Fiordland National Parks, and several adjacent areas, which all told totals about 2.6 million hectares.

National parks protect large tracts of wilderness country, but other types of reserves, not within the ambit of this book though of equal importance, protect smaller areas with special wildlife or wilderness values. The most important of these reserves are on offshore islands – sanctuaries such as Little Barrier Island in the Hauraki Gulf, Maud Island in the Marlborough Sounds and Codfish Island in the deep south – with more stringent protection than national parks (visitors may only go to these islands with a permit). Their main purpose is to provide safe refuges for some of New Zealand's drastically endangered flora and fauna which have been ravaged by the plethora of introduced pests on the mainland. Huge conservation efforts are made to keep these offshore refuges pest free, and to minimise disturbance to native wildlife such as the kakapo, a large flightless parrot on the brink of extinction. Many of New Zealand's distinctive birds are large and flightless like the kakapo, or simply poor fliers, having evolved in a land without mammalian predators and browsers like rats, stoats, possums, cats, dogs, goats and deer – until humans arrived. In addition to limited access reserves, the Bay of Islands, Hauraki Gulf and Marlborough Sounds have other island and coastal reserves of varying status and modification, including recreation

Boulder beach on Little Barrier Island in the Hauraki Gulf, one of New Zealand's most important sanctuaries for native flora and fauna.

and scenic reserves with well developed facilities for visitor enjoyment and education.

None of the reserves in maritime areas extend protection to marine habitats or wildlife, and just as there was a realisation 20 years ago that the national park system neglected lowland areas, there is now a growing awareness that few of New Zealand's underwater ecosystems are safeguarded. A campaign for marine reserves hopes to achieve protection for at least 10 per cent of New Zealand's coastal and marine environment, with equivalent 'no-take' requirements that apply to national park flora and fauna. Progress has been slow, but several marine reserves have been established around New Zealand shores and the Kermadec Islands 1,000 kilometres north-east of Auckland.

The spread of an increasingly urban and materialistic society has meant the protection of large areas of wilderness such as those in our national parks has become vital for the preservation of the planet's biodiversity. National parks have also become an important foil for those New Zealanders, and increasing numbers of tourists, who seek them out for outdoor adventures, or to simply relish the power and beauty of undisturbed nature. Huts and tracks within the parks, some well developed, others rough and remote, offer many opportunities for those who want to get out and enjoy wilderness. Nevertheless, increasing volumes of visitors, and growing pressure from commercial operators with helicopters, aircraft, jetboats, ski lifts and other modern technologies that affect the pristine qualities of wild places, are threatening to destroy the very values that attract people to national parks in the first place. The Department of Conservation, which is charged with guardianship of New Zealand's national parks, attempts to manage these pressures by directing visitors to major attractions, road-end trails and the well-maintained and organised Great Walk network, leaving other regions to their natural processes.

Further issues have been raised by Maori tribes who want to restore their traditional ownership and use rights over national park land or protected native species, threatening to compromise the natural values of some parks. The challenge now is to ensure that the vision of national parks remains intact, and that they are safeguarded as places where the biodiversity of this country can be preserved for present and future generations, where plants and animals can find a safe refuge, and where there is still a chance to experience a natural wilderness that is fast disappearing from the face of the earth.

NEW ZEALAND'S NATIONAL PARKS

FIORDLAND
NATIONAL PARK

Fiordland, the vast wilderness in the far south-west of New Zealand, is the country's largest and the world's fifth largest national park, comprising 1.2 million hectares of mountains, fiords, lakes, forests, river valleys and remote coastline. The promise of exhilarating scenery and pristine wilderness draws people from around the world to walk the Milford Track, gaze across the peaceful waters of Lake Te Anau, or watch in awe as waterfalls drop hundreds of metres down Milford Sound's near vertical cliffs.

Although ice age glaciers are responsible for creating this remarkable landscape, its features are markedly different from the glacial landforms of the Southern Alps to the north because Fiordland's mountains are built from hard ancient rocks of gneiss, granite and diorite. These rocks are far less prone to erosion than the easily shattered greywacke of the Alps, so most of the valleys here retain a classical glacial U-shape, with rounded shoulders that mark the height of former ice flows. The park's 14 magnificent fiords were created by glaciers that flowed west to the sea, while glaciers that flowed east gouged the deep basins filled by Lakes Te Anau and Manapouri, and the park's many other lakes.

The western boundary of the park is a long wilderness coastline indented by deep fiords penetrating 20 kilometres inland on average. Their steep, often near perpendicular

Above: Thought extinct for 50 years, the takahe was confirmed alive, after a number of possible sightings, by an expedition to Fiordland's Murchison Mountains in 1948. The takahe is now the subject of an intensive species recovery programme run by the Department of Conservation. Though the core of the takahe's wild population of 120 still centres in the Murchison Mountains, in recent years the Department has attempted to establish a second population in the nearby Stuart Mountains, with mixed success.

Opposite: Fiordland's greatest icon, Mitre Peak, a splendid and dramatic mountain rising 1,692 metres above the deep waters of Milford Sound.

walls plunge hundreds of metres below the water's surface (up to 450 metres in the deepest basins). These fiords are home to a multitude of marine species, some unique in the world. On the park's eastern boundary, a series of major lakes and rivers stretch in an almost unbroken network from Martins Bay in the north to Te Waewae Bay in the south, collectively forming the largest system of inland waterways in New Zealand. The depth of Fiordland's three main lakes, Hauroko, Manapouri and Te Anau, exceeds 400 metres – the deepest in the country. Between coast and lakes is spread a remote wilderness of broken ridges, peaks and valleys, much of it rarely visited.

Wet Jacket Arm (middle, left) joins Acheron Passage in this view south to Bowen Channel and Long Island – all are part of the complex waterways and islands of Dusky Sound.

Water, a dominant element in the park, appears in many forms, be it in waterfalls, lakes, rivers and fiords, or snow and ice, mist and torrential rain. This is one of the wettest places on earth with over 7,200 millimetres of rain falling in an average year at Milford Sound, fuelled by water-laden westerly weather systems which release their contents on meeting the abrupt mountain barrier (up to 2,000 metres high) along the Fiordland coast. The consequences are often spectacular and sobering: storms send waterfalls plunging down mountain walls, and snow, avalanches and floods frequently block roads and tracks.

This perpetual dampness and wet nourishes the luxuriant, primeval forest that covers two-thirds of the park and forms the largest continuous area of native forest in New Zealand. Beech is the dominant forest, with patches of podocarp and other trees and shrubs. The beech forests here have a distinctive complex multi-layered structure, characteristic of rainforest, and trees are densely covered with wet mosses, liverworts and filmy ferns. At higher altitudes and in many of the park's long river valleys, snow tussock forms a natural grassland, with numerous alpine herbs and plants. In all, 24 plant species are found only in Fiordland National Park.

Fiordland's coastal, fiord, riverine, forest and alpine habitats support an equal richness of wildlife, including many rare and unusual species. For instance, remote tussock country in the Murchison Mountains is the last natural habitat of the large flightless takahe, a bird thought extinct before it was rediscovered here in 1948. A 'special area', with restricted entry, was subsequently formed to protect this remarkable grazing bird. There are only about 120 takahe in the wild, so some breeding pairs have been relocated to mainland facilities and offshore island sanctuaries to improve the species' chances of survival. Other birds which are uncommon or in low numbers elsewhere, but surviving in reasonable numbers within the park, include blue duck, yellowhead, kiwi, crested grebe, New Zealand falcon and South Island robin. Fiordland also has the largest South Island population of the endangered brown teal, probably the most endangered waterfowl in New Zealand. The coastline and the specially protected Solander Islands are habitats for the Fiordland crested penguin, a host of other seabirds, and fur seals. An endemic Fiordland skink is

South Fiord of Lake Te Anau, from the tussock slopes of the Kepler Mountains.

The 580 metre Sutherland Falls above the Milford Track is the highest waterfall in New Zealand, and among the highest in the world.

found on a few small islands and islets. Another distinctive but less obvious feature of this park is its abundant insect, spider and invertebrate life, with more than 300 of the 3000 species present thought to be endemic.

A silver beech in forest in the Kepler Mountains. Fiordland has three species of beech: silver, mountain and red. Silver beech is the most common, growing from valley floor (where it can reach heights of 30 metres) to bushline (where it appears in stunted form between 1–2 metres high). Underneath the tree, with moss hanging from its branches, is New Zealand's native fuchsia, one of the few native deciduous trees in the country.

Fiordland National Park was established in 1952 and one year later the Milford Road was opened, providing access to the park's north-eastern realms. This world famous highway joining Te Anau to Milford Sound passes through spectacular scenery, with many short walks and lookout points along the way. A number of easy walks and day trips also start from Lake Manapouri. Many of the park's half a million annual visitors come to Fiordland National Park just to experience its awe-inspiring scenic grandeur from the side of the highway, while others enjoy guided walks, tramping, kayaking and mountaineering trips, scenic flights, fishing and hunting safaris, or launch outings on one of the park's beautiful lakes or fiords.

For trampers there are three 'Great Walks' in the park. The Milford Track, the most famous of New Zealand's Great Walks, has been impressing tourists since 1889. This four-day tramping trip, which crosses a mountain pass between two valleys from the head of Lake Te Anau to Milford Sound, is renowned for its glacier-carved valleys, alpine flowers, waterfalls and wilderness splendour. Further south, the Kepler Track takes in lake edges, beech forest and the alpine tops of the Kepler Mountains. Lastly, the Routeburn Track traverses above the Hollyford valley and crosses Harris Saddle into Mount Aspiring National Park. Apart from the Great Walks, tramping opportunities in Fiordland are almost unlimited, with over 60 huts and 500 kilometres of tracks, and numerous unmarked routes for the very experienced. But expect rain! Two large designated wilderness areas in the park, the Glaisnock and Pembroke, have no buildings or development, while much of the southern sounds remains underexplored and rarely visited on foot.

Left: Waterfalls triggered by a storm thunder into Milford Sound. New waterfalls appear throughout Fiordland when wet westerly weather systems strike Fiordland's mountains, causing sudden storms that charge its steep mountain catchments with water.

Above: North-east of Mt Tutoko, Grave Couloir, beneath Paranui Peak (2,194 metres) on the edge of the Pembroke Wilderness Area, is a remnant glacier that falls over 1,000 metres from the Ngapunatoru Plateau.

Right: In winter, snowstorms set off 'point release' avalanches that cascade like summer waterfalls down the steep bluffs lining the Hollyford valley. Much larger and more devastating slab avalanches release millions of cubic metres of snow, regularly closing the Milford Highway during winter and spring.

Red and silver beech forest in the Clinton valley, from the Milford Track.

Mackay Falls on the Milford Track near where Mackay Creek joins the Arthur River.

Mt Christina and the Darran Mountains from Key Summit, Routeburn Track.

FIORDLAND NATIONAL PARK

Fiordland National Park
Visitor Centre
P.O. Box 29
Te Anau
Phone: (03) 249 7921

Great Walks Booking Desk
(for Milford and
Routeburn Tracks)
Address as above
Phone: (03) 249 8514

MOUNT ASPIRING
NATIONAL PARK

New Zealand's second largest and least-developed national park is a huge alpine wilderness covering 355,518 hectares of mountains, glaciers and river valleys between Westland and Fiordland. At its heart and always dominating the landscape is the towering 3,027 metre Mt Aspiring, the highest peak outside Mount Cook National Park. From many directions, the mountain has the classic shape of an alpine horn evocative of Switzerland's Matterhorn.

Mount Aspiring National Park extends south of the Haast River to the head of Lake Wakatipu, its southern fringe denoting the end of the Southern Alps and the beginning of the more ancient Fiordland mountain massif. The park's mountains are built of a shining, layered and very friable schist rock that, like the rest of the Southern Alps, had its beginnings as sediment on an ancient seabed, except that here it lay deeper than other sediments and underwent metamorphosis in intense underground 'pressure cookers'. The rocks have since been carved by glaciers and rivers to form the park's present-day landscape. Lakes, moraines, hanging valleys, cirque basins and U-shaped valleys are the legacy of ice age

Sunset colours on the Volta Glacier (above) and (opposite) on the north-western flanks of Tititea/Mt Aspiring (3,027 metres).

glaciers. Most of the 100 or so remnant glaciers in the park are retreating rapidly.

The Red Hills area to the west is a geological quirk where schist gives way to a barren and exposed belt of ruddy coloured 'ultramafic' rocks. The distinctive oxidised colour in the rocks here is because of their high iron and magnesium content. This, and the absence of other vital minerals, inhibits the growth of all but the hardiest of plants. Geologists believe the Red Hills are part of a similar mineral belt found in Nelson almost 500 kilometres north, a striking example of the lateral displacement that has occurred along the Alpine Fault over the last 25 million years.

Mt Pollux (2,542 metres) from the Wilkin valley, a Main Divide peak named Pohaitaka by Maori who in pre-European times lived and followed old trails through the region.

Silver beech is the main forest in the park, with red and mountain beech occurring in southern areas. Rimu, matai, miro and kahikatea mix with silver beech on lowlands west of the Main Divide, where the rainfall is nearly four times heavier than to the east. Above the tree line, the low alpine zone is characterised by a mosaic of snow tussocks, alpine shrubs and herbs such as snow totara, speargrass, mountain daisies and buttercups. Dwarf cushion vegetation, snowbanks, herbfields and fellfields form habitats according to altitude, soils and topography.

Birds are plentiful, especially common species such as rifleman, silvereye, bellbird, fantail and New Zealand pigeon. The park's size and remoteness has also made it a bastion for several threatened species: South Island brown kiwi, blue duck, New Zealand falcon, parakeet and mohua (yellowhead). The Dart forest is a priority site for research into predator

Rusty coloured 'ultramafic' rocks of the Red Hills Range, looking east over the Olivine wilderness towards the triangular summit of Mt Aspiring.

control to protect the mohua. Invertebrates are numerous, and the park shelters 400 species of moths and butterflies, including two species of alpine black butterflies.

A number of the park's rivers are not fed by glaciers and therefore lack the characteristic milky colour of glacial rivers. The Greenstone, Caples, Young and Makarora have clear water, rapids and beautiful pools, and are superb habitats for native fish. Rare species like koaro are present, and the park may be a last refuge for the native grayling. The absence of trout in some rivers adds to their value as habitats for indigenous species.

Maori frequently travelled the valleys and high passes of this part of the country in search of food and greenstone. Later, European explorers, prospectors and adventurers made forays into the wild backcountry, establishing tracks well before the area was declared a national park in 1964. Most renowned of the early explorers were Charlie Douglas and Arawata Bill who made many lone journeys into this country, the latter an eccentric who spent much of his life on his own prospecting for gold, occasionally emerging from the bush to collect provisions or see a doctor.

The area has been most recently popularised by the opening of the Haast Highway in 1960, which cuts across the north-east corner of the park and provides a convenient 'window' into its splendid scenic attractions. Roadside tracks off the highway such as the Makarora Bush Walk, Blue Pools, Fantail Falls and Roaring Billy provide short walks through the park's beech and beech/podocarp forests, frequently ending at picturesque waterfalls. From the highway motorists can appreciate the mountain scenery of the Haast and Landsborough Rivers, both of which flow in wide majestic valleys. The highway provides access to longer tracks up a number of the park's river valleys: the Blue, Cameron Creek, Makarora, Young, Burke and Wills. Other access is from Queenstown and Wanaka where the impressive mountain scenery forms a backdrop to the famous lakes of Wanaka and Wakatipu. Access to the south of the park is via Glenorchy village.

The park offers superb wilderness tramping and mountaineering, particularly as it shares a common boundary with the enormous Fiordland National Park to the south. The most popular tramp is the internationally renowned three-day Routeburn Track. This 32 kilometre Great Walk links Mount Aspiring and Fiordland National Parks via Harris Saddle. Over the summer it is one of the country's most popular tramping tracks, but in winter it becomes extremely hazardous and impassable, with high avalanche danger. All of the park's alpine valleys are magnificent walking country where forest meets grassy river flats

'The Sump' a bottleneck of grey sandstone boulders and fallen trees in the gorge section of the Route Burn, in the Humboldt Mountains. This section of the river is safely bypassed by the Routeburn Track.

framed by snow-covered mountains – the epitome of Mount Aspiring's tranquil beauty. The Rees–Dart Track is a four to five day tramping circuit following the Rees and Dart Rivers through leasehold farmland and the southern part of the national park. The Young, Wilkin and Matukituki valleys have a number of well-used routes, and the West Matukituki valley gives access to Mt Aspiring. Those with plenty of tramping and backcountry experience, as well as a rugged bent, have huge tracts of wild country to explore in this national park. In the remote west of the park is the designated wilderness area around the high plateaux and peaks of the Olivine ice sheet, while even further west the Red Hills Range, which divides the Cascade and Pyke valleys, offers outstanding tramping possibilities through untracked country.

On the Routeburn Track: mountain and silver beech forest, typical of the forests encountered either side of Harris Saddle.

Taking in the view of Lake Harris and the glaciated slopes of Mt Xenicus, from above Harris Saddle.

Grassy valley floors with forest clad sides, like those in the Wilkin valley north of Mt Aspiring, epitomise the park's tranquil beauty.

Heading up the Whitbourn valley towards the Main Divide during a transalpine crossing from the Dart River to the Arawhata valley – one of many wilderness adventures to be had within remote areas of the park.

Right: Climbers during a summer ascent of the north-west ridge of Mt Aspiring, the highest peak outside Mount Cook National Park. For many mountaineers drawn by the mountain's aesthetic appeal, climbing Mt Aspiring by this the most straightforward route is their first experience of a 3,000 metre peak.

Above: The massif of Mt Edward (2,586 metres), above the Dart Glacier, in the south of the park.

Left: One of the delights of the alpine zone here and throughout the Southern Alps is the abundance of flowering plants. The daisy Dolichoglottis scorzoneroides *is often found in wet alpine habitats near 'flushes' where groundwater appears on slopes below ridges or plateaus.*

MOUNT ASPIRING NATIONAL PARK

Wanaka Field Centre
P.O. Box 93
Wanaka
Phone: (03) 443 7660

Glenorchy Field Centre
cnr Oban and Mull Sts
Glenorchy
Phone: (03) 442 9937

Queenstown Field Centre
37 Shotover St
Queenstown
Phone: (03) 442 7933

Great Walks Booking Desk
(for Routeburn and Milford
Tracks)
Address: as for
Queenstown above
Phone: (03) 442 8916

WESTLAND
NATIONAL PARK

Few places in the world can boast unmodified wilderness that stretches from high mountains to the sea, or of glaciers that descend into the realms of temperate rainforest. These distinctions are held by the 117,626 hectare Westland National Park, that within a span of 30 kilometres extends from the snow-covered peaks of the Southern Alps across a narrow strip of pristine forests, rivers, lakes and lagoons to touch the Tasman Sea. It includes many of the country's highest mountains and largest ice-fields as well as magnificent lowland forests and coastline. The park's extensive snowfields feed more than 60 glaciers, of which the longest and most famous, the Franz Josef and Fox glaciers, fall to just 300 metres above sea level.

Westland's mountains are the result of the collision of two of the earth's underlying crustal plates along the Alpine Fault (see Mount Cook National Park), which cuts right through the park at the foot of the Alps and through Franz Josef township. Of the many peaks raised by this collision, Mt Tasman (3,498 metres) is the park's highest. (Although Aoraki/Mt Cook, the highest peak in the country, is just beyond Westland's shared boundary with Mount Cook National Park, it still towers over the Westland landscape.) Glaciers shaped the mountains here as elsewhere in the Alps during the series of ice ages that have

Above: Nesting white herons, or kotuku, on the banks of the Waitangiroto River, north of Okarito, the only breeding site in New Zealand for these beautiful birds. White herons are rare in this country, though common in other parts of the world.

Opposite: Mt Tasman and Aoraki/Mt Cook reflected in Lake Matheson, a few minute's drive from the village of Fox Glacier. Dawn and evening reflections of the Alps in this glacier-formed lake are one of the many memorable sights visitors to the area enjoy.

affected the earth over the past two million years. All the park's lowland landforms too – the moraine ridges, broad valley floodplains, coastal hills and bluffs, the network of lakes and impounded lagoons – are the consequence of repeated advances and retreats of glaciers during the last ice age between 70,000 and 14,000 years ago. At the height of this glaciation, ice sheets extended an estimated 20 kilometres beyond the present coastline, and the sea level was over 100 metres lower.

Sweeping down from the Southern Alps, the Fox Glacier plunges almost 3,000 metres in 13 kilometres towards the West Coast lowlands. This photograph illustrates the narrow choke into which the glacier is forced from its broad tributary snowfields, a factor which along with the steepness of the descent contributes to the rapid speeds the glacier achieves (up to 3–4 metres a day, slightly slower than the Franz).

The wide variety of landforms combined with the past onslaughts of glaciation have created a distinctive and diverse mosaic of forest. Dense podocarp forest, dominated by rimu, cloaks the park's lowlands – South Okarito and Waikukupa have some of highest densities of rimu forests in the country. Kahikatea, New Zealand's tallest tree, grows on wetter flood plains, while rata and kamahi figure on the lower slopes of ranges and montane valleys. Some of the least possum-damaged rata forest left in the country is found in the Copland and Karangarua valleys in the south of the park. One of the impacts of glaciation on vegetation here is the absence of beech. Glaciers wiped out much of the lowland forests, but because beech seed is neither wind-dispersed nor carried by birds, it has recolonised only as far as the park's southern boundary, creating what ecologists call the central Westland 'beech gap'. The park's broad band of sub-alpine forest is dominated by a variety of *Olearia* tree daisies and *Dracophyllum* species which often form a virtually impenetrable thicket. All this vegetation is sustained by the park's renowned high rainfall: over 3,000 millimetres of rain a year on the coast, 5,000 millimetres at the foot of the mountains and 11,000 millimetres on the Main Divide.

The park's diverse habitats support a rich array of wildlife. Okarito Lagoon, a wildlife refuge on the fringe of the park, is one of the largest remaining natural estuaries in the country and a haven for thousands of native and migratory birds. In particular it is the main feeding ground of the royal spoonbill and white heron who breed just north of the lagoon on the banks of the Waitangiroto River. South Okarito forest has the only population of the Okarito brown kiwi, estimated at between 60–100 birds. Rare or uncommon birds in the park include the kaka, kea, whio (blue duck), crested grebe and New Zealand scaup. Among smaller threatened animals are long-tailed bats, Westland skink and a local species of carnivorous land snail. The extensive network of lakes, rivers, streams and freshwater swamps is excellent habitat for the 16 species of native freshwater fish recorded in the park.

Okarito was one of only a few known sites settled in the area by Maori in pre-European times. The gold rushes of the mid 1860s attracted a major influx of European fortune seekers, and by 1866 Okarito and Gillespies Beach had a resident population of 4,000, and a major port had been established at Okarito. As the goldminers moved on, mountaineers and glacier sightseers moved in, and guiding and accommodation businesses sprang up to cater for this upsurge in tourism. Westland National Park was created in 1960 as a park of glaciers and rugged mountains, but after a long and significant conservation campaign against timber milling, the lowland forests and coastal areas of Okarito and Waikukupa were added to the park in 1982.

The park is impressive at any time of year, although wet weather persists in spring and early summer. State Highway 6 bisects the park, and together with various side roads, provides access to the main glaciers, lowland forest walks and glacial features, and to the coast

The upper reaches of the Cook River in the south of the park, below the cloud-swathed La Perouse on the Main Divide. Lyttle Peak is the mountain on the right.

Sightseers in the Waiho valley approach the Franz Josef Glacier, which in recent years has gone against the trend of retreat and thickened and advanced down-valley, reflecting heavy snowfalls several years earlier. Both the Fox and Franz Josef are amongst the fastest flowing glaciers in the world, descending steeply from the Alps to an altitude of 300 metres.

at Okarito and Gillespies Beach. The Fox and Franz Josef glacier terminals are still the main visitor drawcard. Tracks to the tops provide panoramic mountain, glacier and forest views. Also popular are the forest walk to Lake Matheson, and coastal tracks at Okarito and Gillespies Beach. Lakes, coastal lagoons and some rivers and streams are good for kayaking and canoeing, including the meandering Ohinetamatea, said to be the only river in Westland that can be canoed between its inland stretches and the sea in both directions.

For trampers there are tracks to the headwaters of the Copland and Karangarua Rivers. The former is a well used trans-alpine route to Mount Cook National Park, but is most commonly walked as far as Welcome Flat (five to six hours), where there is a hut and hot thermal springs to bathe weary limbs. The most frequently climbed peaks are those above Fox Glacier, while the vast snow basins at the head of the Fox and Franz Josef are also a mecca for ski-mountaineering. As always in the mountains the weather can be severe and change rapidly and only the well equipped and experienced should consider venturing into these realms.

An aerial view of the Southern Alps illustrating its abrupt rise from South Westland's forested coastal plains. The Alpine Fault, where the Pacific and Indo-Australian tectonic plates are colliding and raising the Alps, runs along the base of the foothills. Lake Mueller in the centre lies amid serpentine forest covered moraine ridges that denote former pathways of an ancient glacier that repeatedly advanced and retreated over the plains, depositing vast amounts of eroded debris from the mountains.

The Fox Glacier at sunset near the top of the Fox icefall.

Ferns and mosses and clinging and climbing plants form a chaotic understorey in the kamahi forest encountered on the Minehaha Walk, a short loop track near Fox Glacier.

Lake Mapourika.

Fox Glacier and the western flanks of Mt Tasman.

Three cabbage trees at Gillespies Beach.

Spindly trunks of kahikatea forest on the edge of Lake Wahapo.

WESTLAND NATIONAL PARK

Franz Josef Visitor Centre
P.O. Box 14
Franz Josef
Phone: (03) 752 0796

Fox Glacier Visitor Centre
P.O. Box 9
Fox Glacier
Phone: (03) 752 0796

High peaks of the Southern Alps: (foreground) the three peaks of Mt Haast (3,138 metres), (right) east face of Mt Tasman (3,498 metres), and (left), Aoraki/Mt Cook (3,754 metres).

MOUNT COOK

NATIONAL PARK

Mount Cook National Park is New Zealand's premier alpine park, boasting such attractions as Australasia's highest mountain, the 3,754 metre Aoraki/Mt Cook, and one of the longest glaciers in the world's mid-temperate regions, the 29 kilometre Tasman Glacier. The park covers over 70,700 hectares and stretches 45 kilometres along the eastern flank of the Southern Alps, sharing a common boundary with Westland National Park along the Alp's main dividing ridge. With 26 named peaks over 3,000 metres, 145 named summits higher than 2,300 metres, and permanent snow and ice covering a third of its area, Mount Cook National Park represents the full majestic grandeur of the South Island's mountainous backbone.

The mountains of the Southern Alps are relatively young and still rising; their sedimentary greywackes and schists have been compressed and uplifted as the Pacific and Indo-Australian crustal plates collide deep beneath the surface of the earth along the line of the Alpine Fault. This collision is forcing land upwards at a rate of about five millimetres a year near Aoraki/Mt Cook, and twice as fast closer to the Alpine Fault (which runs west of

Above: On the summit ridge of Aoraki/Mt Cook before the 1991 summit collapse.

the Main Divide at the base of the foothills in Westland National Park). In theory, this rate of uplift should have built mountains the size of Mt Everest. However because the unstable sedimentary rock of the Southern Alps is highly susceptible to erosion, the upthrust has been effectively counteracted.

Among the splendours of Mount Cook National Park is the Mt Cook 'lily', in fact a buttercup (Ranunculus lyallii)*, which flowers in alpine herbfields here and in many other parts of the South Island mountains.*

Glaciers are another major force shaping the park's landscape. Beginning their journey in huge snow-collecting basins high in the mountains, these rivers of frozen water act like giant conveyor belts carrying eroded rock down the mountains, scouring the landscape and depositing the rubble as moraine. The cirques and sharp aretes of mountain basins and ridges, and distinctive U-shaped valleys are all the handiwork of glaciers. During the ice ages, numerous glaciers extended well beyond the present park boundaries and onto the Mackenzie Basin, depositing ridges of moraine that today mark their ancient routes. Lakes Pukaki and Tekapo fill depressions shaped by glacial ice thousands of years ago. The amount of rock moved by these glaciers is immense – the Tasman River flows on sediments at least 500 metres thick dumped by glaciers over the past 50,000 years. Rubble covers the lower reaches of the Tasman Glacier as the ice continues its work of transporting rock from the mountains. Milky coloured rivers and streams laden with ground up rock flour pour from glacier terminals; the park's ten main glaciers feed the headwaters of the large braided river systems of the Tasman and Godley Rivers. These rivers change course across gravel-strewn valleys time and again, and slowly fill the lakes of the Mackenzie Basin with the products of glacial erosion.

Lenticular clouds form over Aoraki/Mt Cook and Lake Pukaki as a nor'west storm develops over the Southern Alps.

The park's high altitude and harsh climate result in a vegetation that is predominantly alpine, and pockets of beech forest at the lowest altitudes soon give way to cold-tolerant alpine herbfields, shrublands and tussock grasslands. Alpine herbfields display colourful flowers from mid-November till the end of February. Of these, the giant buttercup, the Mount Cook 'lily', largest of the world's buttercups, is the highlight. Several rare, endangered and a few endemic species inhabit this inhospitable alpine country. Even on the highest rocks of Aoraki/Mt Cook, 14 species of lichen survive, and the higher altitudes are home for a number of endemic insect species. Over 40 species of birds are also found, at least for part of the year, in the demanding high mountain and valley environment. The kea, New Zealand's mischievous mountain parrot, is one of the most memorable.

Maori regard Aoraki/Mt Cook as an atua (god), a fact recognised in the recent landmark settlement between the Ngai Tahu tribe and the New Zealand Government. Among other things the agreement acknowledged the special relationship Ngai Tahu have with the mountain. Mt Cook's Maori name, Aoraki, honours the eldest son of Rakinui the Sky Father in Maori legend. Another translation of Aoraki is 'cloud in the sky'. Three New Zealand amateur climbers were the first to scale Mt Cook's summit on Christmas Day 1894, and Mt Sefton was conquered the following year. The Mount Cook region has been a popular destination for sightseers and mountaineers for some 130 years, and a number of hotels, lodges and huts have been built in the area, often not long surviving the ravages of fire, flood, wind and ground instability.

Aoraki/Mt Cook from the north at sunrise, with the South Island's main dividing ridge in the foreground.

The park's spectacular scenery is readily appreciated by any visitor to Mount Cook Village, where Mt Sefton and The Footstool tower over this tiny hamlet that serves as the park's headquarters. A variety of short walks from Mount Cook Village or the nearby Tasman Valley Road lead to small tarns, alpine forest and splendid glacier and mountain lookouts. A one hour walk to the Sealy Tarns affords views of the Hooker Valley and the triple-peaked massif of Aoraki/Mt Cook. Popular longer trips are a day walk up the Hooker Valley to the terminal lake of the Hooker Glacier, and the half day Ball Shelter Track which gives superb views of the Tasman Glacier.

The park's mountains are regarded as the best mountain climbing country in Australasia, despite their unstable greywacke rock and frequent avalanches, whose threatening rumble is especially common in winter and early spring. Although Aoraki/Mt Cook is the ultimate conquest, other peaks like Sefton, La Perouse, Dampier, Tasman, Malte Brun and

Elie de Beaumont offer challenging and rewarding climbs. There are 17 huts in the park, ranging from small bivouacs with no facilities to large, fully equipped buildings. Alpine routes are serious undertakings and only for the experienced and properly equipped. Fierce storms can arrive with little warning, winds can gust up to 235 kilometres an hour, snow can fall at any time of year, and temperatures can drop rapidly.

Snow skiers have long been lured to the snow basins and glaciers of the Mount Cook Region, and skiing is still a favourite activity today. Skiing on the Tasman Glacier attracts the greatest numbers, but those with mountaineering skills often favour ski-touring in quieter snowfields away from the noise of aircraft. Cross-country skiing in winter on lower, safer terrains such as the Hooker Valley is also popular. Aerial sightseeing (often including a glacier landing), or just absorbing the awe-inspiring scenery and exhilarating mountain environment around Mount Cook Village, are other attractions for the more than 200,000 visitors to Mount Cook National Park each year.

The view north along the Main Divide from the summit of Mt Tasman and down onto the Tasman Glacier.

First light touches the summit of Mt Sefton (3,157 metres), viewed from Mueller hut in the south of the Park. Reaching Mueller hut involves a steep ascent from Mount Cook village, but it is nonetheless a popular location with enticing views of Sefton's east face and Aoraki/Mt Cook. Simple mountain shelters such as these have been used as bases for mountaineering in the park since last century. These modern huts now have bunks, cooking stoves and emergency radios.

Wintry beauty at Mount Cook village after a south-west snow storm, on the track below Governor's Bush, one of a number of short walks in the vicinity of the village.

South face of Aoraki/Mt Cook from the Hooker River. Mt Hicks is the prominent dome at left.

Winter in the Hooker valley.

Morning light on Mt Tasman, second highest of New Zealand's mountains, above the Grand Plateau and the top of the Hochstetter icefall.

MOUNT COOK NATIONAL PARK

Mount Cook National Park
Visitor Centre
P.O. Box 5
Mount Cook
Phone: (03) 435 1819

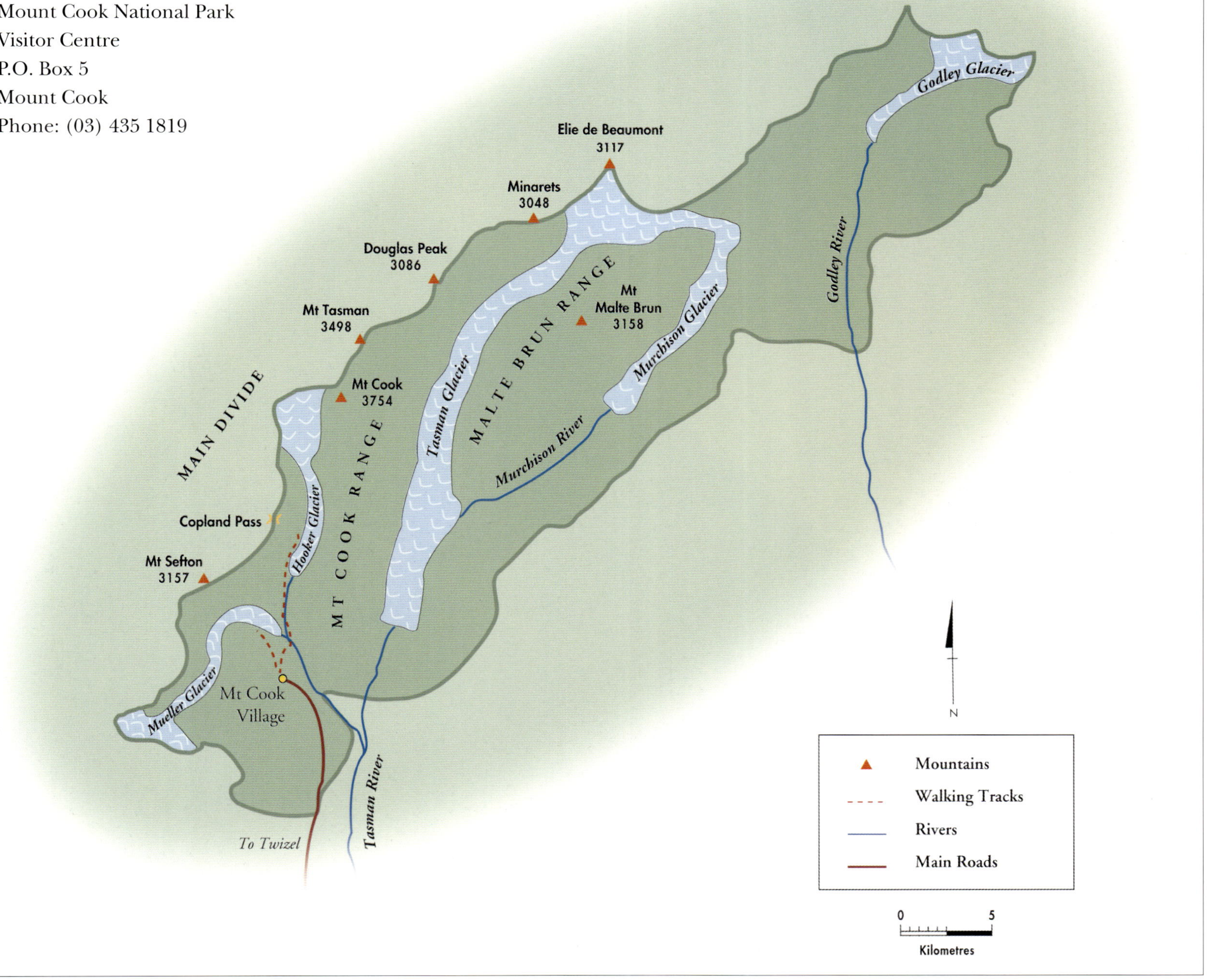

ARTHUR'S PASS

NATIONAL PARK

Straddling the Main Divide of the Southern Alps, Arthur's Pass National Park is an alpine park whose rugged snowcapped peaks, glaciers and alpine meadows rise high above steep gorges, bush-clad slopes and wide river valleys. One of the park's most striking features is that the high peaks and mountainous passes of the Alps cut the park into two dramatically contrasting halves, each with a very different climate and vegetation. The east is covered with a uniform mantle of beech forest broken by wide shingle riverbeds, and, being sheltered from the prevailing westerly storms by the mountains, has a drier warmer climate. The west, recipient of the heavy loads of rain that sweep in from the Tasman Sea (over 5,000 millimetres falls annually at Otira in the west compared with an average of 1,500 millimetres at Bealey in the east), is cloaked in a luxuriant rainforest, with a lush understorey of shrubs, ferns and lichens. Between these two very different environments, the alpine regions of the park present yet another very different habitat, with icy mountain peaks, glaciers, tussock basins, tarns and alpine meadows.

The Southern Alps have been raised by a process of uplift that has lasted two million

Above: The Devils Punchbowl Falls, a 150 metre fall about a one hour return walk from Arthur's Pass village.

Opposite: River cascade in the upper Otira valley, an alpine area easily reached from the Arthur's Pass Highway, providing access to, among other peaks, Mt Rolleston.

years. During the recent ice ages, huge glaciers extended west from the Arthur's Pass mountains to beyond the West Coast's present shore, and east across the Canterbury Plains. As the glaciers retreated, they left the legacy of U-shaped valleys, alpine tarns, narrow rock ridges and ice-smoothed bedrock that today give the park its characteristic grandeur. Erosion, earthquakes and avalanches have further dissected the mountains into a labyrinth of ranges and valleys, moving millions of tonnes of rubble and fashioning extensive scree slopes, sprawling shingle fans and broad river terraces.

The headwaters of the Waimakariri River emerge from the Arthur's Pass mountains, flowing eastwards along the path gouged by a large ice age glacier.

The wide range of altitudes, climates and the park's east/west split creates a great variety of habitats and abrupt changes in vegetation and animal communities. Most eastern slopes and flats, from the valley floors to the bushline, are covered with mountain beech forest. But across the Divide in the higher rainfall zone, the forests suddenly become wet and luxuriant. On higher slopes grow rata and mountain totara, while on the lowlands tall podocarp trees flourish alongside kamahi and quintinia. The brilliant red flowers of the rata are ablaze in the Otira Gorge during January and February. The ferny understorey of the western forests is also noticeably different from that of the drier eastern beech forests.

Above the bushline sub-alpine scrub again shows a marked difference between the east and west sides of the Main Divide, being much denser and more species diverse in the west. Eastern vegetation at this height by comparison is sparse and dominated by *Dracophyllum* and snow totara. At even higher altitudes, snow tussocks, alpine grasses and herbs endure in the harsh mountain climate. Splendid displays of sub-alpine and alpine plants and flowers are relatively accessible from tracks off the highway near Arthur's Pass.

Common forest birds are the bellbird, fantail, brown creeper and grey warbler. Yellowhead and robin are found only in eastern regions, and the tui only in the west. The great spotted kiwi can be heard at night around the Arthur's Pass township, and during the day the inimitable kea are often seen too. The park is incredibly rich in invertebrate fauna, and has been a favourite study area for entomologists since the 1850s.

The park includes most of the headwaters of the Waimakariri and Otira Rivers, and some tributaries of the Taramakau River system. Together, these rivers virtually bisect the South Island from east to west. Wide shingle riverbeds are frequently flooded, and have only a sparse vegetation, while the open braided rivers of the Waimakariri and Poulter are nesting grounds for birds such as the wrybill and black-fronted tern.

Maori crossed mountain passes in this area while transporting pounamu (greenstone) from Westland to Canterbury. Today the Arthur's Pass Highway is the main route over the Main Divide (and at 920 metres is the highest road over the Southern Alps). Travelling this road in itself affords a fine glimpse of the park's attractions as well as providing easy access to the park's valleys and alpine areas. The visitor centre in Arthur's Pass township is the focus for visitor information and park interpretation, and is a useful base for people making short visits to the park. There are railway stations at Otira and Arthur's Pass with daily passenger services between Greymouth and Christchurch.

There are many opportunities for visitors to enjoy the alpine environment of Arthur's Pass. With 16 named peaks over 2,000 metres, the park is popular for mountain climbing even though much of the rock is unstable greywacke and argillite. Mt Rolleston (2,275 metres) is the most accessible of the park's mountains and can be climbed in a day from Arthur's Pass. Mt Murchison at 2,408 metres is the highest. Many mountain routes are only

Southern rata flowers are a brilliant red contrast against the deep-green rainforest on the wetter western side of Arthur's Pass. Flowers of both northern and southern species of rata are a spectacular feature of the South Island's western forests throughout summer.

Mt Oates (2,009 metres) on the drier eastern side of Arthur's Pass, above the braids of the Edwards River.

climbed in winter, and climbers should be knowledgeable in mountaineering techniques and avalanche assessment. Avalanches occur throughout the year.

The park is excellent tramping country, with a large choice of tracks and routes that link valleys on either side of the Alps with Main Divide crossings. Some alpine passes are within the reach of average trampers, while others are for the more experienced. The weather however is severe and unpredictable, and can be cold and wet even in the middle of summer. Much of the rain falls in short, high intensity storms and as much as 250 millimetres can fall in 24 hours, turning rivers into swollen torrents that can be extremely dangerous to cross.

Day walks of either a few hours' or a day's duration lead to forests, waterfalls, alpine meadows and mountains. The Devils Punchbowl Falls at 131 metres is a popular one hour return walk from Arthur's Pass Village. Steep tracks from the village lead to 360 degree views of the park's mountains. Temple Basin skifield, hunting and fishing draws many enthusiasts to this area.

Crossing snowfields above the White River, below Mt Murchison.

Traversing a snow ridge after a mid-winter ascent of Mt Murchison, the highest peak in the park.

The kea (Nestor notabilis), *a mountain bird renowned for its inquisitiveness around humans. Although kea spend a lot of time above the bushline, it nests in mountain forests, usually in rock crevices or old trees.*

ARTHUR'S PASS NATIONAL PARK

Arthur's Pass National Park
Visitor Centre
P.O. Box 8
Arthur's Pass
Phone: (03) 318 9211

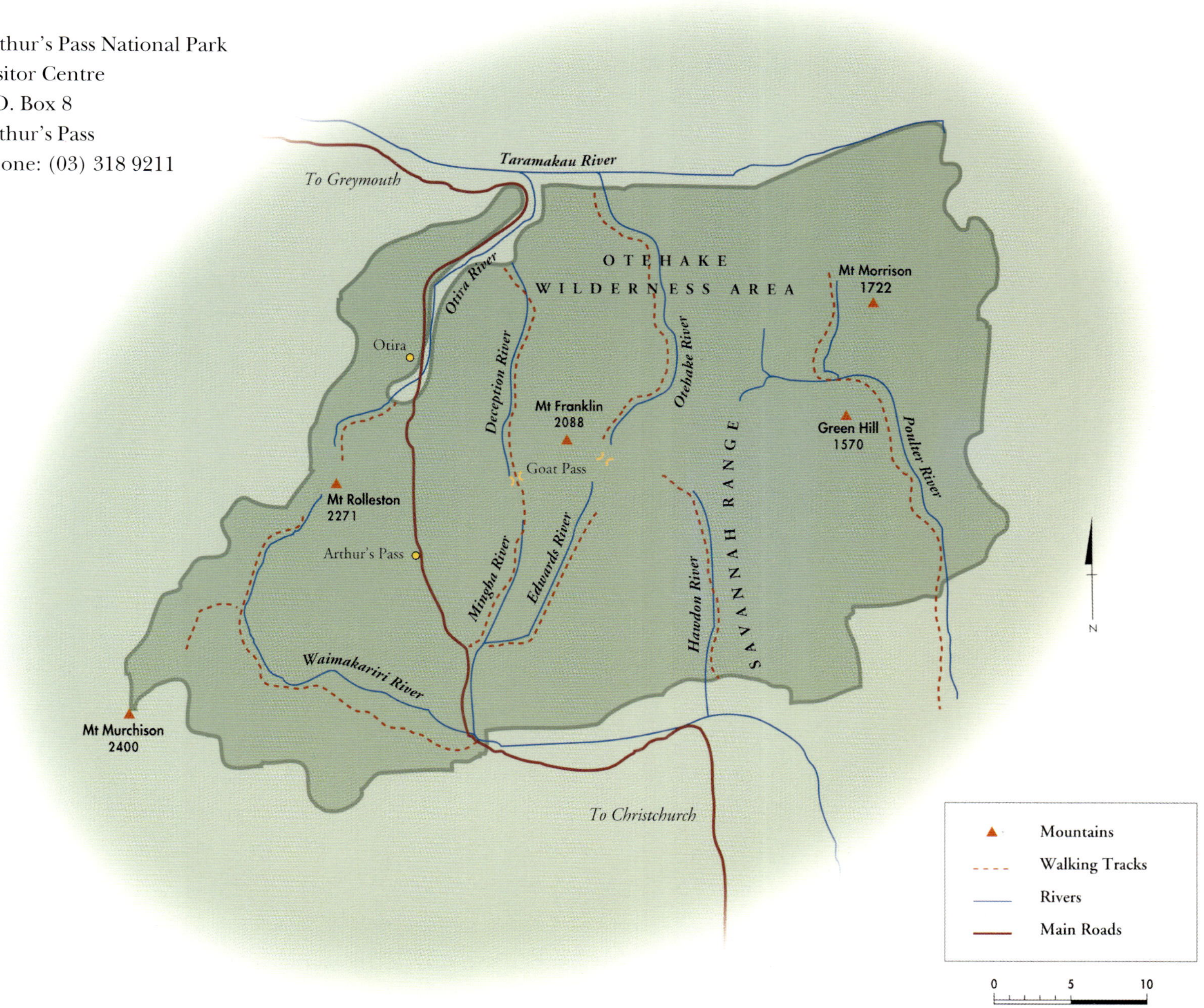

PAPAROA
NATIONAL PARK

Behind the popular tourist stopover of Punakaiki's pancake rocks and blowholes lies a spectacular limestone landscape that extends from the coast to the edge of the Paparoa Range. The diverse lowland forests, sculpted rock and underground cave systems of this area went virtually unnoticed for years until plans to log the area in the 1970s led to a vigorous conservation campaign, and eventually to the creation of the Paparoa National Park in 1986.

At the centre of the park is a huge area of warped limestone lying in a depression between the ranges and the sea. Over millions of years earthquakes and erosion have buckled and carved the soft and water-soluble limestone rocks into an extraordinary landscape. On the coast, the powerful swells of the Tasman Sea have sculpted limestone, sandstone and granite into towering bluffs, precipitous headlands and intricately detailed rock formations with blowholes and platforms such as those found around Dolomite Point at Punakaiki. Inland, rivers flowing west from the mountains have chiselled the limestone into deep chasms and canyons with vertical walls, sometimes hundreds of metres high, complete with large natural arches and overhangs, columns, turrets and alcoves. Streams suddenly disappear underground, leaving dry streambeds and blind valleys on the surface

Above: The lady's slipper orchid Dendrobium cunninghamii, *one of six native epiphytic orchids in New Zealand.*

Opposite: Lowland forest in the Pororari valley.

while the water flows on in subterranean channels carving the underground rock into complex cave systems with shafts, passages and galleries. Water droplets work further wonders in the underground limestone caverns, and over thousands of years have formed stalactites, stalagmites and other remarkable calcite decorations. Some of the more impressive of the park's subterranean creations are the five kilometre Xanadu cave system, and the 41 metre Cataract Pot. Inland of the limestone plateau is a broad shallow limestone syncline or depression with further intriguing variations on the landforms of the coastal limestone belt.

Approaching the limestone canyon and lush coastal broadleaf forest in the Pororari valley. A good walking track leads up this valley, one of the few that venture into the park's interior.

The extensive karst landscape is covered in a dense lowland forest that is largely unmodified. The mild climate, fertile soils and heavy rainfall of this region have made this a diverse and luxuriant forest, where podocarps like rimu and miro thrive together with a broadleaf understorey of kamahi, quintinia and toro. The inland Porarari Basin has at least 25 different forest types, from almost pure stands of kahikatea forest to stunted associations of rimu, silver pine and toatoa on leached infertile soils. Along the coast, northern rata and groves of nikau palms, nearly at their southern limit, create a sub-tropical atmosphere and form a canopy over an intense tangle of supplejack vines and creeping kiekie. A very rare self-draining swamp (polje) lies at the northern end of the Bullock Creek farm, privately owned but totally enclosed by the national park.

The mosaic of forest types growing on the limestone supports the highest concentrations of native forest birds so far recorded in the South Island. Tuis, bellbirds, pigeons, tomtits, grey warblers, fantails and silvereyes are all commonly seen. These forests are one of the last strongholds of the great spotted kiwi, which is abundant here. Other threatened species in the park include the kaka, blue duck, a number of giant land snails and a locally endemic alpine weta. There are also likely to be rare or threatened species of lizard, invertebrates and cave fauna present. The rarest bird in the park is the endemic Westland black petrel, a large land-burrowing and nesting bird which has its only breeding site in New Zealand on the Punakaiki coastline.

Limestone boulders on the coast near Punakaiki.

Although the Paparoa Ranges beyond the park's eastern boundary are not high (1,300–1,500 metres), they are extremely rugged. The granite and gneiss rocks of the ranges are some of the country's oldest (in contrast with the young limestone rocks of the lowlands) and have been shaped by ice into a chain of low craggy mountains with pinnacles, towering bluffs and deeply gouged cirques. Thick beech forests and impenetrable sub-alpine scrub cloak the slopes of the ranges, and frequent cloud and rain (200 days a year on average, with 8,000 millimetres falling annually on the crest of the ranges compared with 2,000 millimetres on the coast) contribute to the range's very different character to the lowland limestone belt.

The Paparoa/Punakaiki region was one of the earliest places to be settled on the coast by Maori, who were attracted by the area's abundant fish, birds and edible plants. From the 1860s, parts of the Paparoas were heavily prospected and mined during the West Coast gold rushes. In 1867 the Razorback Road (now the Inland Pack Track) was cut through the lowlands to provide an alternative to the treacherous coastal route. This was used until early this century, when the completion of the Westport–Greymouth Coast Road in 1929

A stream cascades over a bed of waterworn limestone in the Paparoa syncline.

provided easy access to what is one of the most scenic and dramatic coastlines in New Zealand, and opened up the area to a new breed of visitors.

Seaward end of the Miko Cliffs, Perpendicular Point.

Punakaiki's attractions of layered limestone 'pancake rocks', surge pools and geyser-like blowholes (especially impressive in westerly weather conditions) have long been a major attraction, drawing 300,000 visitors a year. But even more natural wonders are in store for those who venture further off the road into the national park. Several short walks start at or near Punakaiki. Trumans Track is an easy stroll through a superb sample of sub-tropical coastal forest, emerging at a wild coast with cliffs, caverns, blowholes and a waterfall. The Fox River cave is an easily and safely visited limestone cavern with a 200 metre passage decorated with calcite formations. Other walks follow river valleys into the magical heartland of the park, with beautiful rock pools suitable for swimming, spectacular limestone gorges and rock formations, and disappearing and reappearing streams. Some of the park's finest limestone features can be seen up the Fox River and its tributaries. A large limestone overhang known as the Ballroom is a seven to eight hour return trip.

Although the park has a limited range of longer tracks and routes, the 27 kilometre Inland Pack Track gives good access to the interior of this surreal landscape. This two to three day route has no huts, but there are camping sites and rock overhangs for shelter. Deep potholes and sinkholes riddle the landscape, often well hidden by the thick forest mantle, so extreme care should be taken in exploring this country and visitors are strongly advised not to wander off the marked tracks.

Pancake Rocks blowhole in action during a westerly swell at Dolomite Point near Punakaiki.

Patterns of tidal erosion on a mudstone shore platform near Seal Island.

Limestone reflection in the Fox River canyon.

Waggon Creek, a tributary of the Fox River.

PAPAROA NATIONAL PARK

Paparoa National Park
Visitor Centre
P.O. Box 1
Punakaiki
Phone: (03) 731 1893

Jetty at Kerr Bay, Lake Rotoiti, and Mt Robert on the skyline.

NELSON LAKES
NATIONAL PARK

Nelson Lakes National Park is a 101,872 hectare wilderness of rivers, valleys and mountains that embraces the northern end of the Southern Alps. The lakes from which the park derives its name are the two elongated and beautiful lakes, Rotoiti and Rotoroa, which form impressive northern entrances to the park beneath a backdrop of mountains and beech forests.

The bedrock of the park's landscape is almost exclusively sandstone and greywacke that has been lifted with the rest of the Southern Alps along the Alpine Fault. The fault runs through the north-west of the park, and is exposed in the Speargrass valley and at St Arnaud. In recent ice ages, great glaciers advanced from the mountains towards the Tasman Sea, gouging depressions that, when the ice later retreated, filled with water to become the eight kilometre long Lake Rotoiti and 15 kilometre Lake Rotoroa. The glaciers also carved many of the park's features, such as its arete peaks.

When the glacial ice began retreating between 10,000 and 14,000 years ago, beech forest recolonised the park to become the main forest. All four species of beech are present

Above: The rare blue duck, or whio.

– red, silver, black and mountain – usually in association with one another or kamahi. Three vulnerable species of beech mistletoe are found here, but otherwise there are few unusual plants in the park, which has landscapes and ecosystems that are typical of much of the Southern Alps. There is little true lowland forest in the park, although a few small stands of podocarps are found on river flats and lake edges. At higher altitudes beech trees become stunted and covered with moss and lichen, creating a fairytale atmosphere, especially when branches are laden with winter snow. Above 900 metres the alpine tops support diverse plant life across a wide range of habitats including tarns, wetlands, fellfields and rocky outcrops, tussock and alpine meadows.

South and eastern faces of Mt Travers (2,338 metres) from Travers Saddle, at the head of the Travers valley. The saddle is crossed during the Travers–Sabine circuit

These high regions are playgrounds for the boisterous kea and habitat for flocks of pipits and two species of giant land snail. Lower down, the park's large continuous tracts of beech forest are important for many common forest birds, along with threatened species such as the South Island kaka and yellow-crowned parakeet. But here as in other South Island beech forests, the ecosystems supporting native wildlife are being severely degraded by the population explosion of wasps accidentally introduced from Europe. An 800 hectare 'mainland habitat island' has been established on the St Arnaud Range in an attempt to return at least a part of the park's ecosystem to a more or less natural state. Such islands are intensively managed to reduce introduced plants and animals, offering the hope that

Looking east from Robert Ridge to the cloud-covered St Arnaud Range, in winter.

species like the kaka, already under severe threat from rats and stoats, can survive on the mainland – initial success with kaka breeding has proved very encouraging.

Lakes Rotoiti and Rotoroa are among the largest lakes outside Fiordland National Park with virtually unmodified catchments. The exceptional clarity of the waters of both lakes allows unusually pristine plant communities to grow to a depth of 80 metres; extensive freshwater mussel beds also grow on the lake beds. Lake Rotoroa has significant wetlands on its shores, including flaxlands and sedgelands near the outlet, and kahikatea forest that is periodically inundated by floods.

High camp by a tarn in the east Sabine valley, looking north towards Mt Cupola (2,263 metres).

Valleys and passes in the park were used by early Maori settlers who followed trails between Nelson, Marlborough, the West Coast and Canterbury. Nineteenth century European explorers such as Brunner, Heaphy, von Haast and Travers then utilised the knowledge of Maori guides in their journeys through these parts of the South Island, and today trampers can retrace the footsteps of these early travellers, enjoying solitude little changed since last century.

This is a relatively low key park, with no one big attraction or 'Great Walk' to draw large numbers of visitors and commercial operators with aircraft and vehicles. The park's valleys, mountain tops and lake edges are easily accessible by a variety of tracks, and within a short time visitors can be immersed in the leafy quiet of a beech forest, gazing over tranquil lake waters, or enjoying the wide vistas of a bushline lookout. There are many short walks and day walks: from St Arnaud, the circuit of Lake Rotoiti and the Mt Robert Ridge walk, both about six hours, or the shorter St Arnaud Ridge walk, are all good opportunities to experience a range of the park's natural attractions. Tramping trips of two to five day's duration often involving a loop or return walk through forested valleys and over easy alpine passes are popular. Most tramping trips start from the two lakes or the main river systems that feed into them – the Travers into Lake Rotoiti and the Sabine and D'Urville into Rotoroa. Traversing Robert Ridge to Lake Angelus is a popular two-day tramp, while the Travers–Sabine Circuit is the most popular long tramp, a four to seven day journey. Along the western boundary the Matakitaki and Glenroy valleys are less often visited but by no means inaccessible. Remoteness increases up successive valley systems from the Travers in the north-east to the Glenroy in the south-west. The route south over Waiau Pass links with the St James Walkway outside the park. For mountaineers the higher peaks in the park rise well above 2,000 metres and offer moderate climbing challenges. The Mt Robert skifield is a small but locally popular winter destination, reached by a two to three hour tramp. Lakes Rotoiti and Rotoroa are both easily accessible, and are ever-popular holiday areas for picnicking, boating, water sports and year-round trout fishing. While Lake Rotoiti is favoured because of its proximity to St Arnaud village, Lake Rotoroa is valued for its undeveloped and peaceful character. Recreational hunting is a popular sport throughout the park (permits are available from the Department of Conservation), and the upper valleys, especially around Blue Lake, are valued chamois hunting territories.

Lake Constance and surrounding mountains at the head of the West Sabine river.

Opposite: The leafy green of a red beech forest in the Sabine valley, typical of valley floors in many areas of the park.

The boughs of a large old beech tree, in mountain forest near Blue Lake, sprawl across the west branch of the Sabine River.

Mountain and silver beech forest at Blue Lake.

High on the slopes of Mt Hopeless a climber looks north toward Angelus Ridge where large snow avalanches have cut swathes through the montane zone beech forests.

NELSON LAKES NATIONAL PARK

Nelson Lakes National Park
Visitor Centre
Private Bag
St Arnaud
Phone: (03) 521 1806

KAHURANGI
NATIONAL PARK

New Zealand's newest and second largest national park, the 452,000 hectare Kahurangi National Park, lies in the north-west corner of the South Island and is probably best known for its Heaphy Track, walked by thousands of visitors each year. Kahurangi means 'treasured possession' and, true to its name, the park protects mountain ranges, lowland forests and coastline that together represent the greatest variety of landforms, habitats, plants and animals of any of New Zealand's national parks.

This remarkable area is the most geologically complex and varied in New Zealand. Huge belts of hard grey granite run through western areas and on the border of the park in the east, while the remainder of the park's bedrock consists of some of New Zealand's oldest sedimentary rocks. Over hundreds of millions of years, including three phases of mountain building (the last of which remains active today) these belts of rock have time and again been uplifted, eroded, folded, faulted, metamorphosed and intruded by other material. The oldest landforms in New Zealand are the park's peneplain landscapes (over 50 million years old) represented in the park's expansive areas of rolling downs – Gouland Downs, Gunner Downs and Mt Arthur Tablelands. Also within the park are sizable regions of considerably younger waterworn limestone – these areas together with the much older

Above: Sun orchid (Thelymitra *sp.*)

Opposite: Mosses and ferns mass on a matai trunk in the lush podocarp/beech forest found in the Oparara valley, north of Karamea.

though similarly waterworn marble (a metamorphosed limestone seen in the Mt Arthur and Mt Owen regions), form one of the most extensive karst landscapes in the country with characteristic bluffs, arches, sinkholes and caves. Other rocks contain New Zealand's oldest fossils and longest sequence of fossil records, covering some 220 million years. Throughout the park huge earthquake slips testify to the ongoing process of tectonic movement in this region; the biggest of these slips dammed rivers and created large lakes such as those found in the Karamea valley.

Boulder Lake, with the Dragons Teeth, a feature of the Douglas Range, on the distant skyline. This area is on the edge of the 87,000 hectare Tasman Wilderness Area.

One of the factors that has made this part of the country so extraordinary is that by and large it escaped the great ice sheets that covered other parts of the South Island during the ice ages. Not only did ancient peneplain landscapes survive, but plants and animals found refuge here while similar terrain elsewhere was covered with ice. For example, the high limestone plateaux of Garibaldi Ridge and the Matiri Range in the south-west avoided the worst of the glaciations and are now a treasure house of plant life, supporting some 500 plant species, almost half the total flora of the region. The lesser impact of glaciation, combined with the diversity of rocks, soils, altitudes and climatic conditions has contributed to the evolution of a remarkably diverse flora and fauna, with a high number of endemic species.

Over 1,200 plant species are found in the park, amounting to nearly half New Zealand's native plants, including one-third of all tree, shrub and climber species, and an exceptional 80 per cent of New Zealand alpine species. Eighty-five per cent of the park is forested, a mosaic of upland beech forests in eastern and central parts of the park, while lowland and coastal forests of mixed podocarp, beech and hardwood species dominate in the west. On the West Coast just inland from Karamea lies the limestone country of the Oparara Basin, with some of the densest stands of rimu forest in the South Island. A little further north, a rich and diverse lowland forest grows in the Heaphy Basin, influenced by a milder coastal climate. Unbroken sequences of habitats and vegetation types join the western coastline with the alpine tops, such sequences being uncommon now in modern

New Zealand. In the alpine areas above the coast, rolling downlands with their cover of red tussock, umbrella fern and wire brush stand out as clear patches amidst surrounding beech-clad granite and limestone. Unusual communities of pink and yellow pine, cedar and *Dracophyllum* also grow on upland granite.

Over 100 native bird species, including many scarce or uncommon species such as the great spotted kiwi, rock wren, fernbird and yellow-crowned parakeet, inhabit forests, wetlands and alpine zones. Amongst invertebrates are 'living fossils' like the giant land snail (the park protects two-thirds of the *Powelliphanta* genus) and the biggest New Zealand spider, the Nelson cave spider, which inhabits limestone caves underneath Oparara's lowland forests. The significance of this region as an ice age wildlife and plant refuge became clear when it was discovered that Honeycomb Hill cave in the Oparara valley contains an internationally important collection of sub-fossil bird and reptile remains, including those of now extinct native birds dating back 20,000 years.

Maori settled in coastal areas of the park and frequently used coastal trails and probably crossed the ranges along the route now followed by the Heaphy Track. This was named after Charles Heaphy, a European draughtsman and adventurer who, with Thomas Brunner

Stunted beech, southern rata and other sub-alpine plants on the Gouland Downs, the ancient peneplain landscape traversed by the Heaphy Track between Golden Bay and the West Coast.

Nikau palms rustle and sway in the constant winds that blow across the Heaphy coastline on the park's west coast.

and Maori guide Kehu, explored much of the West Coast in the mid 1800s. The Heaphy and Wangapeka Tracks were upgraded to pack tracks between 1888 and 1899 to link Golden Bay and Karamea. Many other tracks in use today were established by goldminers and graziers trying to earn a living from the area in the latter half of the nineteenth century.

Top Arch, one of a series of spectacular limestone archways that occur on the Oparara River, centre of an area of forested limestone in the west of the park.

This legacy of tracks has benefited wilderness trampers, hunters and anglers who are well catered for in Kahurangi, which has over 500 kilometres of tracks and 50 huts. Although there are numerous short walks and day walks from road ends near Karamea, the Cobb, Aorere and Wangapeka valleys, and Mt Arthur's Flora carpark, the real delights of this park are enjoyed on longer tramps into the park's interior. The 82 kilometre Heaphy Track is one of New Zealand's Great Walks, a four to six day trip that traverses a range of landscapes. The Wangapeka Track, south of the Heaphy, can be walked in conjunction with the Leslie and Karamea valley tracks to link with the Mt Arthur Tablelands, or instead combined with the Heaphy Track to create a round trip between Nelson and the West Coast. For the wilderness adventurer the 87,000 hectare Tasman Wilderness Area in the Tasman Mountains has no huts, tracks or other development.

Kayakers and rafters show increasing interest in the Karamea River, a challenging three to four day journey which is graded four to five in difficulty (on a scale of six). Complex, long and deep cave systems, particularly those in the Mt Arthur Range and beneath Mt Owen, attract experienced cavers from throughout the world. Above ground, Mt Arthur and the Oparara Arches near Karamea are within reach of most people who want to appreciate the incredible waterworn forms created in a marble/limestone landscape.

Sub-alpine forest on the Mt Arthur Tablelands, with the snow-covered Twins on the Mt Arthur Range in the distance.

The glaciated marble landscape near Mt Owen, in the Marino Mountains, on the eastern side of the park.

Beech forest on the banks of the Oparara River.
Overleaf: Sea foam is blown onto the western beaches next to the Heaphy Track.

KAHURANGI NATIONAL PARK

Department of Conservation
Private Bag 5
Nelson
Phone: (03) 546 9335

ABEL TASMAN
NATIONAL PARK

With its mild and sunny climate, curving beaches of golden sands, large tranquil lagoons and forest-covered hills on the edge of turquoise seas, Abel Tasman National Park is a pocket of coastal paradise. This is New Zealand's smallest national park, protecting nearly 23,000 hectares of coastline and high country hinterland between Golden and Tasman Bays. It is also the country's most modified national park, but although some of its forests have been felled and rock quarried from its coastline, its natural beauty casts a spell over its many visitors. Along the coast sweeping golden beaches and large tidal lagoons stretch between small coves and forested headlands; inland, beech forests cloak the hills, surrounding cascading rivers, waterfalls and bush-fringed pools; and in the high country of the south-west the marble landforms of the Canaan Downs create a dramatic, almost alien landscape.

The park's landforms are built mainly of coarse granite rock, with a steep interior carved by small but vigorous rivers. On the coast, sea, wind and rainwater attack the composite granite, splitting apart its mica, feldspar and quartz to expose crystalline surfaces

Above: A greenhood orchid, a member of the Pterostylis *species.*

Opposite: Sunrise over Awaroa Inlet, a large tidal lagoon at the north end of the park.

which eventually break down into the sparkling golden sands that are a characteristic of the park. High on the park's western boundary, the Canaan Downs form a surreal landscape of infertile marble and schist, where patches of bush abut open expanses of fluted marble and tussock. Through the centuries, rainwater, which is naturally acidic, has steadily hollowed out the marble of this region into a honeycomb of caves, tunnels and shafts. Harwood's Hole, the deepest sinkhole in New Zealand, drops 176 metres into the centre of the Takaka Hill.

Sea-worn granite boulders at the mouth of an estuary. Sparkling quartz, feldspar and mica eroded from the park's granite bedrock are massed together by the sea to create the golden beaches (see below) for which Abel Tasman is most famous.

Once entirely covered with podocarp rainforest on the few fertile lowlands, and beech at most other levels, the park's vegetation has suffered more than a century of land clearance, fires and milling. Most of the park's forests are in various stages of regeneration, though the thin infertile soils of the granite bedrock mean this process is slow. The low fertility soils also mean that there is a low diversity of plant and bird life in the park. Beech is the main tree, and all five species of New Zealand beech find a place that suits them across the park's range of altitudes – from sea level to 1,000 metres. The forest is richest in the damp gullies near the coast, with a lush understorey of leafy trees and shrubs, tree ferns, kiekie and supplejack. Black beech covers the dry ridges and headlands near the sea, with hard beech in the moister interior. Kanuka and manuka lead the regeneration process in areas where recent windfall or fires have destroyed the mature forest. Above 350 metres red and silver beech become the main trees, generally mixed with kamahi, quintinia, toro and southern rata. Silver beech dominates the higher forests of the park. The karst landscape in the west of the park has its own distinct flora and fauna, including the giant land snail *Powelliphanta*.

Totaranui beach, fringed by coastal forest, is a popular destination at the northern end of the Coast Track.

Many of the forest birds that would once have found shelter in the forests of this area have disappeared – tui, bellbird, pigeon and fantail are the main survivors. The threatened marsh crake, bittern and banded rail are found in coastal wetlands, while the park's rocky shores are one of the few sites for the rare reef heron. Inaccessible (to browsing animals) rocky promontories are also one of only

While many walk the Abel Tasman's famous Coast Track, sea kayaking is an enjoyable alternative which offers the opportunity to investigate the rock stacks, reefs and islands offshore, as well as many small mainland coves and bays not accessible on foot.

two known localities for a species of native coastal peppercress plant (*Lepidium banksii*).

Offshore islands and stacks are also included within the park. The rodent-free and relatively unmodified Tonga Island provides a refuge for native species that have disappeared or are rare on the mainland, such as whau, taupata and the large leaved milk tree, and the burrowing little blue penguin. Fur seals are found on the more remote granite headlands of Tonga Island and Separation Point. A recently created marine reserve in the vicinity of Tonga Island complements the national park and will hopefully allow a part of the underwater environment to be restored to its natural state.

The gentle and varied coastline attracted early Maori settlers to the area and the remains of six fortified sites and several villages have been recorded here. A dramatic and bloody first encounter between Maori and European occurred off the park's coast in 1642 when the first European explorer to reach New Zealand's shores, the Dutchman Abel Janszoon Tasman, arrived in Golden Bay. Several of his crewmen died in the skirmish and Abel Tasman sailed away without ever setting foot on New Zealand shores; 300 years later he became the namesake of this park and its creation in 1942 was timed as part of the tricentennial celebrations of Abel Tasman's visit. Unlike most of New Zealand's national parks which are preserved in their natural and unmodified state, Abel Tasman National Park tells the story of most of New Zealand's history since human arrival – settlement by Maori, timber extraction, ship building with the fine New Zealand timbers (at Awaroa and Torrent Bays), exploitation of local rock (granite from Tonga Bay was used to build the Nelson Cathedral steps and Wellington Post Office), and clearance of the forests for farmland. In the early 1900s the charms of the coastline attracted bach owners who dotted the small bays with holiday homes. One such bach owner, conservationist Perrine Moncrieff, initiated a successful campaign for the establishment of the national park to prevent further logging in the area.

A granite rock stack at Anapai Beach, north of Totaranui.

The gentle terrain and climate make the park easily accessible for people of all ages in all seasons. Thousands of visitors each year walk the 51 kilometre Coast Track, an easy three to five day 'Great Walk' through coastal forest beside idyllic sandy beaches and across large tidal inlets and estuaries. Inland routes link the coast with the park's higher reaches, including the karst landscape around Canaan Downs, and Moa Park where a small depression supports the park's only alpine plants. There are several short walks starting from or near the park's main entry points: Totaranui, Marahau, Torrent Bay and Canaan. The many opportunities for camping, walking, fishing, sailing and sea-kayaking make this the most popular holiday coast in the South Island in summer, and wonderful to visit when less busy in spring, autumn or winter.

Southern fur seals are a common sight along the coast, particularly on the park's granite headlands. Shallows around Tonga Island, centre of the Tonga Island marine reserve, provide a nursery area for young seals.

Te Pukatea Bay (foreground), and Anchorage and Torrent bays, a quintessential example of Abel Tasman's crescent beaches and rocky headlands.

Sand patterns in tidal flats near the entrance to Awaroa estuary.
(Opposite) The mixed beech and podocarp forest near Awaroa.

Spotted shags roost on coastal granite cliffs. A complex of layers, faults and shapes in the rock has been exposed by sea, wind and rain erosion. These same erosive forces have shaped the rounded boulders, shore platforms and rock stacks that typify the coastline.

ABEL TASMAN NATIONAL PARK

Department of Conservation
Private Bag 5
Nelson
Phone: (03) 546 9335

WHANGANUI
NATIONAL PARK

Steeped in Maori and European history, the Whanganui River is both namesake and central feature of Whanganui National Park. New Zealand's longest navigable river begins its 290 kilometre journey high on Mt Tongariro, flows west to Taumarunui and then turns south to enter the Tasman Sea at Wanganui. In its central reaches, south of Taumarunui, the Whanganui carves a winding path through rugged hills cloaked with one of the largest tracts of lowland native forest left in the North Island – it is this striking landscape (74,231 hectares) that is now protected in Whanganui National Park. Although the river and its bed are not actually included in the park, some 170 kilometres of the river flows through it – drifting by boat or raft through fern-clad gorges and mist-wreathed, forested valleys is many visitors' experience of this region.

The park's landforms are comparatively young, built of sandstones, siltstones and mudstones deposited as marine sediments and lifted above sea level about one million years ago. Vulnerable to rapid erosion, these soft sedimentary rocks, called 'papa', have been attacked by the rainfall (about 1,700 millimetres annually) and incised and dissected by numerous rivers and streams, resulting in a landscape of sharp ridges, sheer bluffs, deep narrow gorges and spectacular waterfalls. Erosion is still an active force today, visible in the

Above: Canadian canoes tethered to the shore outside a park hut at the end of a day's paddling.

Opposite: Mamaku, the New Zealand tree fern, line the banks of the Whanganui River.

Whanganui River's muddy sediment-loaded waters, or when whole sections of forest sheer off and plunge into the river, leaving exposed papa cliffs.

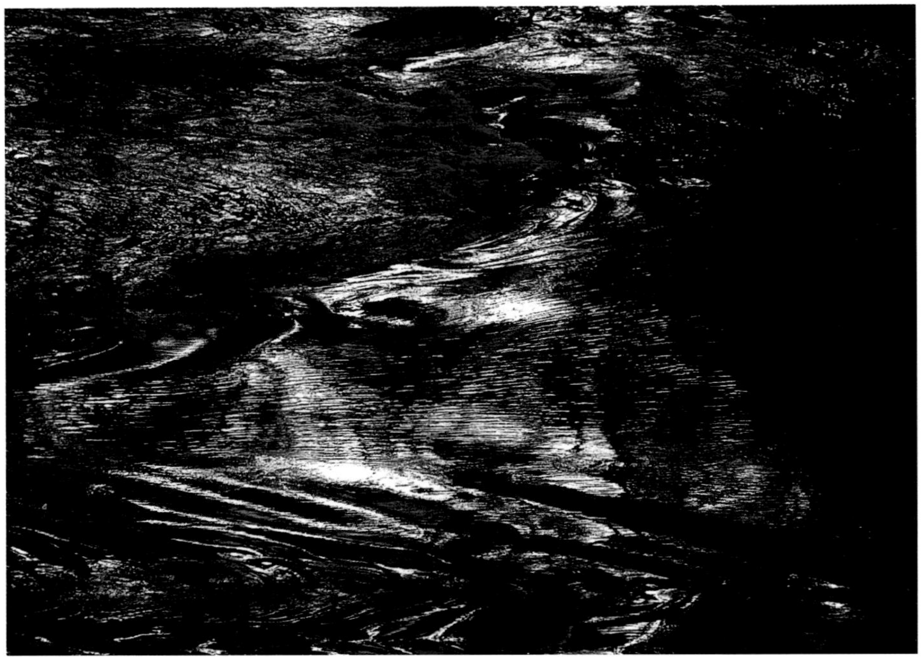

The darkening moods of a river rapid.

Softening the sharp edges of this landscape (which poet Denis Glover described as crumpled like an unmade bed) are the park's extensive native forests. Fertile lowland flats covered with volcanic ash support a diverse podocarp/broadleaf forest featuring rimu, northern rata, rewarewa, pukatea, kamahi and kowhai. Tawa is the most common tree. Beech dominates in the thin sedimentary soils of hills where the fertile ash has been eroded off, and the distinctive dark foliage of black beech is frequently seen on crests of narrow ridges. Communities of ferns, sedges and herbaceous plants cling to the damp sides of river gorges. A special feature of the vegetation is the native herb parataniwha, which grows more profusely here than anywhere else in the country.

The forests and rivers are habitat for a variety of wildlife, including most species of North Island native forest birds. There are large populations of robin and the nocturnal brown kiwi, and lesser numbers of yellow-crowned parakeet, New Zealand falcon, whitehead and kaka. Rifleman, kereru, pied tit, tui, bellbird, fantail, grey warbler, kingfisher and silvereye are widespread. The endangered blue duck, or whio, lives on some rivers, especially the Manganui o te Ao, a tributary of the Whanganui River and the location of a lengthy study of the duck's ecology. Rivers are home for a variety of indigenous fish, including eels, lamprey, galaxid (whitebait) and koura (freshwater crayfish). Numerous sightings have been made of long-tailed bats, mainly along the Whanganui River.

Maori legend tells how the Whanganui River filled the trench carved by Mt Taranaki when he fled from the Central North Island after warring with mighty Tongariro. Maori have lived along the river's edge for over 600 years – the river provided not only a link to spiritual and legendary worlds, but also, thanks to its ease of navigation, a practical link between the Central North Island and the western coast and hinterland. Local tribes named every major rapid, and significant bends had a kaitiaki or guardian who controlled the mauri, or life force, of the place. Eel fishing was (and still is) popular and weirs were constructed where river currents converged. A number of pa and kainga (villages) were located at sites within the national park. When European settlers arrived, many attempts were made to farm the banks of the mid-Whanganui. (The great majority of farms were abandoned and have now been reclaimed by bush.) The river became an important transport route for European settlers too, and a popular riverboat service was established in the 1890s, carrying settlers, tourists, mail and freight. At its peak around the turn of the century the riverboat tourist service had 12 boats and an international reputation. During this era, attempts to protect the Whanganui's native forests for their high scenic value resulted in the creation of the area's first reserves.

The Whanganui River is the main accessway to the national park, and centre of most recreational activities. It is the most canoed river in New Zealand with over 4,000 people paddling its waters each summer. Notwithstanding the 239 rapids between Taumarunui and the sea, it is classed as a beginner's river suitable for novices. Within the park, huts and campsites are provided along the river, and in summer the use of these facilities is managed as the 'Whanganui River Journey' by the Department of Conservation, similar to a 'Great Walk'. Rafting and jetboating are alternative ways to enjoy the river and to reach the park's forested interior for tramping or hunting (hunting of pigs, goats and fallow deer is encouraged during specified hunting seasons).

New Zealand's wood pigeon, the kereru.

The Whanganui River slips quietly through a landscape of tall tree ferns and dense podocarp forest on steep mudstone banks.

Of all New Zealand's national parks, Whanganui is the most closely associated with human settlement and there are a variety of historic sites. Mementos of the riverboat era can be seen in the restored *MV Ongarue* at Pipiriki, and in landings and ringbolts on the banks, and training walls – rock groynes in shallow areas that channelled water to make the river deep enough for riverboats to pass – on the river bed. The intriguing 'Bridge to Nowhere' provides one of the last visible remains of abandoned European settlement. Much of the park is rugged and undeveloped, but there are a number of short walks and day tramps, and two 3–4 day tramping routes – the Matemateaonga Walkway and the Kaiwhakauka-Mangapurua Track – each about 40 kilometres in length. The Atene Skyline Walk is a popular day walk, and short walks can be enjoyed at Te Maire, Maraekowhai, Pipiriki and Atene. Taumarunui is a starting point for exploring the Whanganui National Park for many river adventurers, and is a focus for interpretation of the park and its attractions. The historic settlement of Pipiriki is another gateway, particularly to the wilderness reaches of the Whanganui River.

Land cleared for settlement and farming after World War I has slowly been reclaimed by the forest, although relics of the period like the 'Bridge to Nowhere' remain, and are now protected within the park as historic structures. The bridge is used by trampers on the Maungapurua Track.

Over 4,000 people a year canoe the Whanganui River between Taumarunui and Pipiriki, one of the few multi-day river journeys in New Zealand suitable for novice canoeists. Paddling the river is also one of the best ways to experience the park.

WHANGANUI NATIONAL PARK

Department of Conservation
Private Bag 3016
Wanganui
Phone: (06) 345 2402

Pipiriki Field Centre
RD 6
Pipiriki
Phone: (06) 385 4631

Taumarunui Field Centre
P.O. Box 50
Taumarunui
Phone: (07) 895 8201

EGMONT
NATIONAL PARK

Encircled by a wide mantle of deep-green forest, the graceful cone of Te Maunga Taranaki (also known as Mt Egmont) is the majestic centrepiece of Egmont National Park. Maori legend tells how Taranaki once stood in the Central North Island with his fellow mountain gods Tongariro, Ruapehu and Ngauruhoe. When he was defeated in a fight with Tongariro over the beautiful Mt Pihanga, Taranaki fled westward to the coast where he now stands alone and isolated, his forested slopes rising 2,518 metres above the surrounding ringplain.

Mt Taranaki is the latest expression of a chain of volcanoes that have erupted in the region over the last two million years. Its cone is of the same andesitic rock as Mt Fuji in Japan, and has a symmetrical shape characteristic of young andesitic volcanoes throughout the world. Two older, extinct and much-eroded volcanoes, Kaitake and Pouakai (once a similar height to Taranaki), lie to the north-west and are also protected within the park. Taranaki itself has been built, collapsed and rebuilt in a series of eruptions that began about 120,000 years ago, with the volcano's present cone forming some 20,000 years ago. Since the 1775 eruption, when small amounts of ash were dumped on its upper slopes, the volcano has lain dormant. Taranaki's slopes, although from a distance appearing relatively

Above: Alpine shrubs typical of sub-alpine zones on the mountain.

Opposite: Mt Taranaki (2,518 metres) from the north-west, with the Pouakai Range – the eroded stump of an extinct volcano – in the foreground.

even, are broken by bluffs, lahar mounds and deeply incised ravines.

More than 300 streams and rivers radiate from the mountain's slopes, providing a constant supply of water to the surrounding fertile ringplain, which was formed by the vast quantities of debris that were dumped onto it during Taranaki's eruptions. Maori began clearing the land that would eventually be developed by Europeans into one of the North Island's most productive farming areas. The extent of forest clearance was a catalyst for the formal protection of the mountain in 1881 when all the land within a radius of 9.6 kilometres of the summit was made a forest reserve. In 1900 the area became New Zealand's second national park – an island of natural wilderness surrounded by a sea of pastoral farmland.

Mt Taranaki from near Holly hut, looking up Minarapa Stream, which contains the best preserved lava flow on the mountain. Below the summit is the lava block known as the Turtle, while lower down is one of a number of domes on the mountain formed by a bubbles of viscous lava emerging through fractures in the underlying strata.

The park's vegetation is influenced both by its island-like isolation from other North Island forests, and by wide variations in altitude and climate (with frequent alternations between settled and stormy weather and continually changing winds). Diverse rainforests grow on the lowland margins, dominated by kamahi and huge scattered rimu and rata. Higher, kamahi and totara form a 'goblin forest', assuming tangled, stunted shapes draped with ferns and mosses, and clinging liverworts and lichens. Beyond 1,200 metres, fragile alpine herbfields and meadows of tussocks and native grasses survive on the exposed mountain heights. The lower slopes of the Kaitake Range are covered in forest dominated by tawa, an echo of the forests that were widespread on the ringplain before human settlement.

The variety of native plants overall is small, perhaps because the volcano is relatively new on the landscape, and because of its isolation from other North Island forests. Beech for example is noticeably absent. However, the park is the only North Island location for a number of species, including mountain ribbonwood and *Polystichum cystostegia*, an alpine fern. Possums and goats have had devastating impacts on the forest in some areas of the park, prompting programmes to reduce these introduced pests.

Because it is the only large tract of native forest in the region, Egmont National Park provides a home for many of the district's native wildlife. As well as common birds like the bellbird, kereru and rifleman, some of the more unusual and threatened species here include the North Island brown kiwi, fernbird, and New Zealand falcon. Blue ducks have bred after being successfully reintroduced to the park. Some invertebrates are endemic to the park's forests and forest margins. New Zealand's largest terrestrial amphipod ('hopper') is found only in this park, as is a distinctive form of giant land snail.

Mt Taranaki is sacred to local Maori (the mountain's tapu on its higher reaches was lifted as recently as 1979), and the saying *Ko Taranaki te Maunga* (Taranaki the mountain) is said to signify the peak's unity and perfection in Maori eyes. The mountain has numerous sites where chiefs were buried; on the Kaitake Range over 30 occupation sites have been recorded. Maori also occupied places on the lower slopes of the Pouakai Range and on Taranaki.

Easily accessible by three sealed main roads, Egmont National Park is today popular with both day visitors and those seeking a longer backcountry experience. Picnics, scenery and short walks can be enjoyed near the road ends, each of which has visitor facilities: the

Mt Taranaki in early winter, from the south. In the foreground is the subsidiary cone Fanthams Peak, while the prominent point right of the summit dome is aptly called the Sharks Tooth. Lava flows have formed conspicuous ridges, bluffs and valleys that splay from the summit in a radial pattern.

Cordyline indivisa, *the broad-leaved cabbage tree, or toii, a relative of the more commonly seen cabbage tree* (Cordyline australis) *in lowland parts of New Zealand.*

North Egmont Visitor Centre and the Camphouse at Egmont Road, the Stratford Mountain House and Manganui Skifield on Pembroke Road, and the Dawson Falls Tourist Lodge, Dawson Falls Visitor Centre, and Konini Lodge on Manaia Road. There are numerous easy bush walks from the road ends, and to the bushline. Those wanting longer and more challenging adventures can explore the more than 140 kilometres of walking and tramping tracks in the park, or climb to Taranaki's summit. A circuit of the mountain (usually a three to five day hike) and the Pouakai Range attracts fitter trampers. There are nine huts for overnight use, and one historic hut – 'Old Syme' on Fanthams Peak – which is the oldest recreational hut in Taranaki, and one of the few remaining huts in the country whose materials were carried to the site on peoples' backs.

A young New Zealand tui.

Mt Taranaki is covered with snow in winter, and snow and ice climbing, and skiing at the small Manganui Skifield, are popular activities. Rock climbing is enjoyed in summer. Care is needed above the bushline at all times as the weather can be harsh and changeable. Taranaki's summit is usually a straightforward climb in summer in good conditions, but in winter ice and rapidly changing weather make climbing the mountain hazardous – ice axes, crampons and appropriate clothing are essential. Mt Taranaki is the most climbed mountain in New Zealand, but it also has the highest death toll!

Sub-alpine shrub and grasslands above Kahui hut on Taranaki's western slopes, from the track around the mountain.

Kamahi forest interior, typical of the renowned 'goblin forests' of the montane zone.
Overleaf: Bells Falls where the Stony River cascades over a 31 metre bluff near Holly hut.

EGMONT NATIONAL PARK

Stratford Field Centre
RD 21
Stratford
Phone: (06) 765 5144

North Egmont
Visitor Centre
RD 6
Inglewood
Phone: (06) 756 8710

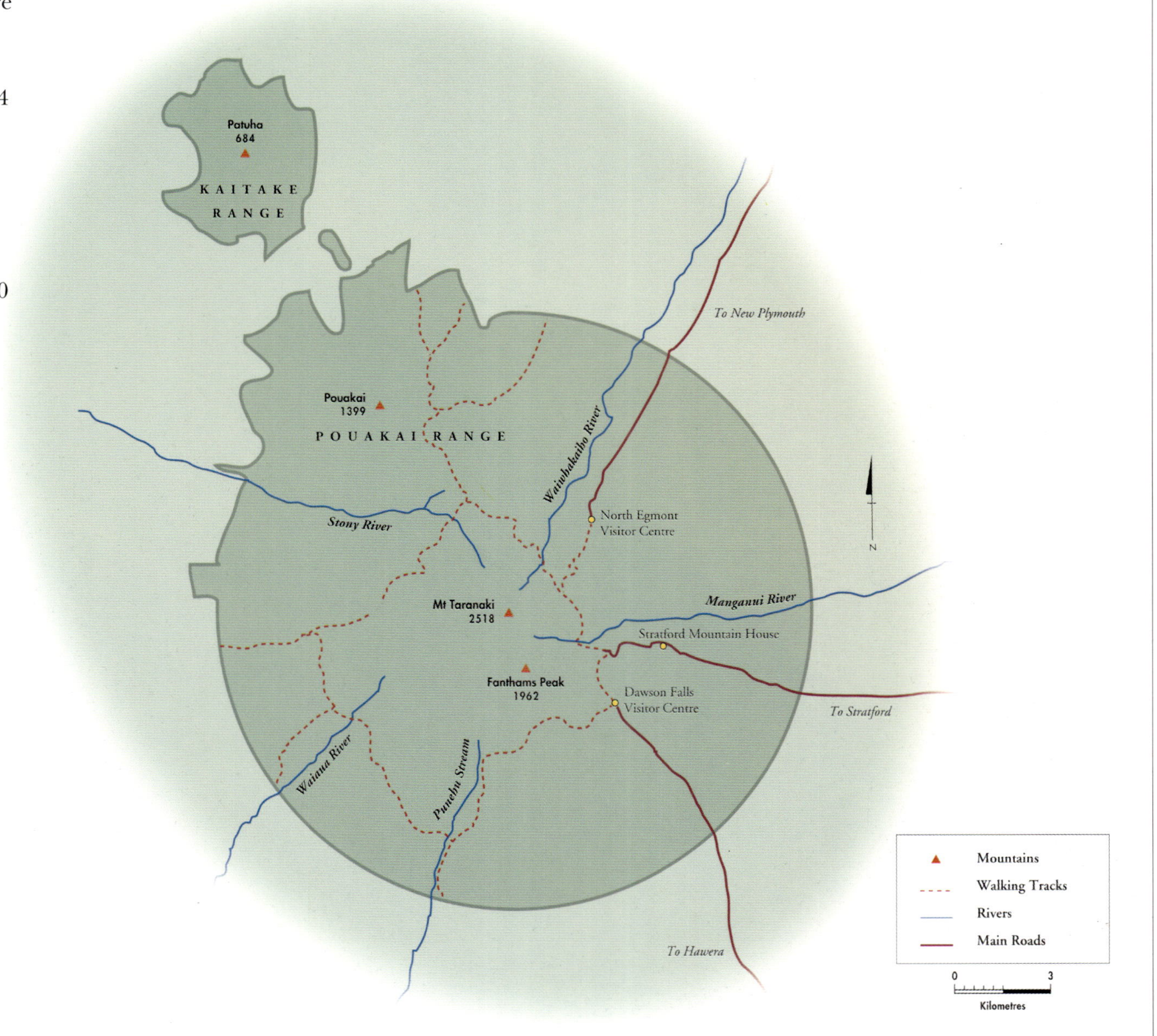

Ash and steam clouds boil skywards and are then blown north during the June 1996 eruption from Mt Ruapehu.

TONGARIRO
NATIONAL PARK

This spectacular volcanic park in the Central North Island was New Zealand's first national park, and the fourth to be created in the world. The park is centred around two large active volcanoes, Mts Ruapehu and Tongariro, with the high cone of Ngauruhoe forming part of the latter's volcanic massif. In 1988 the park was declared a World Heritage Site for its natural landscape values, and five years later given dual world heritage status in recognition of the special cultural significance of the mountains to local Maori tribes.

Tongariro National Park lies at the southern end of a zone of active volcanism that stretches from Mt Taranaki in the west to White Island off the Bay of Plenty coast, and on to the Kermadec Islands and Tonga. This zone is part of the 'Pacific Ring of Fire', a ring of volcanic and earthquake activity along the edges of the huge Pacific crustal plate. Quieter expressions of this volcanic hot spot are the frequent ash showers from Ngauruhoe, and Tongariro's Ketetahi Springs and the still steaming fumaroles of the Te Maari and Red Craters. At the other extreme, geologists believe the cataclysmic AD 186 eruption from the crater now filled by Lake Taupo, just to the north of the park, was responsible for wiping out most forest in the region as well as flinging ash over the North Island. This devastating eruption was six times as large as the 1863 Krakatoa eruption in Indonesia.

Above: Ngauruhoe, the smaller and younger subsidiary cone of Tongariro, and the much older Ruapehu massif.

The volcanoes of Tongariro National Park have been built during many phases of volcanic activity. Ruapehu, the North Island's highest peak at 2,797 metres, erupted as recently as 1996. In a spectacular show the mountain blasted steam and ash hundreds of metres into the air, coating the surrounding towns and countryside. Ruapehu's famous crater lake, one of the few hot crater lakes in the world that is surrounded by permanent glaciers and snowfields, and certainly one of the more accessible of the world's hot crater lakes, quite literally boiled over, sending torrents of mud and water (lahars) rushing down the mountainside. Ngauruhoe, the classically shaped cone south of Tongariro, is the youngest and most continuously active of the park's volcanoes – its last significant eruption in 1954 resulted in 'strombolian fountains of lava', lava flows and ash showers.

Tama Lakes, the water-filled craters between Ruapehu and Tongariro.

In general the park experiences a cold climate, and in winter is a place of deep snow, high winds and icy temperatures. Remnant glacial tongues extend down Ruapehu's main valleys to around 2,000 metres. The wide range of climatic conditions and continuous volcanism have greatly affected the park's vegetation, making it one of the most dynamic natural landscapes in New Zealand. In repeated cycles large tracts of vegetation have been obliterated or burnt – the Taupo eruption of AD 186 destroyed all forest in the northern and eastern parts of the park. In more recent times human inhabitants have also started fires. These natural and human-induced processes of change have created a landscape of forests, tussock, desert, and boulder and gravel fields. Much of the park's central region is regenerating tussock, woody shrubs or flax. Other non-forested areas of the park, including the upper slopes of all the volcanoes and the lower eastern slopes of Ruapehu (the Rangipo Desert) where the climate is severe or the soil poor, nevertheless provide habitats for some of the most interesting plants and plant communities in the park.

Below the bushline, much of the park is clothed in tall beech forest, with smaller areas of podocarp/broadleaf forest at lower altitudes particularly on the western slopes where there are better soils and a milder climate. Over 550 species of native plants are found in the park, at least 80 per cent of which are endemic to New Zealand. The New Zealand falcon and kereru are frequently seen, and North Island kaka may be sighted on the slopes of Ruapehu. Blue duck are found in Ruapehu's south-western catchments, while banded dotterel are common on lower altitude scree slopes during the summer breeding season. There are isolated populations of brown kiwi. Long-tailed bats are also present in the park, and a major population of short-tailed bats was rediscovered early in the 1990s.

Ruapehu and Tongariro are mountains sacred to the Maori, especially to the Tuwharetoa and upper Whanganui River tribes who have lived in the region for almost 1,000 years. In 1887, to protect the tapu status of the summits of his mountains, the paramount chief of Tuwharetoa, Te Heuheu Tukino IV, gifted the sacred summits to the Crown, saying *"The mountains of the south wind have spoken to us for centuries. Now we wish them to speak to all who come in peace and in respect of their tapu."*

Tongariro National Park hosts more visitors (nearly one million each year) than any other in New Zealand. Major attractions are the country's two largest commercial skifields, Whakapapa and Turoa, and with its good system of tracks the area offers excellent tramps and short walks. The Tongariro Northern Circuit, one of New Zealand's Great Walks, winds

Decaying stumps are all that's left of a grove of kaikawaka (mountain cedar) amongst beech forest near Whakapapa. Threatened by ash fallout, lava or fire, forests have a tenuous existence in Tongariro's volcanic landscapes. Other environmental factors contribute to the death of forest trees – why the kaikawaka above died is not known.

Ruapehu's steaming crater lake, photographed in April 1996, still surrounded by ash from eruptions in October 1995.

over Mt Tongariro and around Mt Ngauruhoe, and can be enjoyed as either a day trip or a three to four day tramp. For those seeking a more remote backcountry experience, the round the mountain track provides a four to five day hike around Mt Ruapehu. Both tracks can be walked at any time of year, though summer months are safest for these journeys. The Tongariro Crossing is a popular full day tramp over varied volcanic terrain that includes Tongariro's Red Crater, emerald-coloured lakes and the hot springs of Ketetahi (visitors are asked to respect the fact the springs are on Maori land). Whakapapa is the starting place for several other day-long or shorter walks. A mantle of permanent snow and ice covers the tops of Ruapehu to around 2,000 metres, making mountain climbing and ski-touring popular activities, although like any other mountain region winter presents particular hazards from avalanches and bad weather.

Ngauruhoe (2,291 metres), Tongariro's southern outrider, is the youngest and most active of all the volcanoes in the park, erupting on average every two to seven years. Shaped in the classic cone form of an andesite volcano, Ngauruhoe is believed to have begun erupting onto the landscape 2,000 years ago. The last major eruption involving lava flows from the volcano was in 1954.

One of Tongariro's emerald lakes, more prosaically known as a 'parasitic pit crater'.

Red Crater on Mt Tongariro is still active; its last eruption was in 1925.

The June 1996 eruption of Mt Ruapehu.

The large flax wetland north-west of Ruapehu.

Volcanic debris and isolated plants on the Rangipo Desert; Mt Ngauruhoe on the horizon.
Opposite: Beech forest interior on the round-the-mountain track near Mangaehuehu hut.

Right: Tawhai Falls on the Whakapapanui River cascades over a lava bluff near Whakapapa Village on the northern side of Mt Ruapehu. The falls, reached by a short walk from the road, are a popular challenge for canoeists.

Above: An old buttress-rooted beech tree near Lake Rotopounaumu, just north of the park, thought to have survived the AD 186 eruption from Lake Taupo which incinerated most of the park's forest. Beech would have recolonised from such refugia, though it is slow to spread because its seeds are neither dispersed by birds, nor carried far by wind.

Left: The nocturnal native forest owl, the ruru, or morepork, is the only indigenous owl in New Zealand. It is most active in the twilight hours, or on moonlit nights, and is often heard calling out its 'more pork' call. Owls have acute sight for hunting and very sensitive hearing.

TONGARIRO NATIONAL PARK

Whakapapa Visitor Centre
c/- Post Office
Mount Ruapehu
Phone: (07) 892 3729

Ohakune Field Centre
P.O. Box 10
Ohakune
Phone: (06) 385 8578

Korokoro Falls, a short distance up the Korokorowhaitiri Stream from the Lake Waikaremoana Track.

TE UREWERA
NATIONAL PARK

Te Urewera National Park is a vast forested wilderness in one of the remotest regions of the North Island. Located in the hinterland dividing Central North Island and East Cape, Te Urewera has a reputation as a powerful, mysterious and spirit-filled landscape, with precipitous terrain, mist-filled valleys, and the evocative Lake Waikaremoana lying in its midst. This dramatic landscape has been inhabited for much of the last thousand years by Maori tribes, including the Tuhoe, 'The children of the mist', whose spiritual and cultural traditions remain closely linked with the park's forested hills and lakes. Te Urewera is also the North Island's largest national park and forms part of the biggest continuous tract of forest left in the island.

A rugged and unyielding area, its three main ranges, the Ikawhenua, Kahikatea and Huiarau, are part of the North Island's 700 kilometre mountainous backbone that extends from Wellington to the East Cape. Built mainly of ancient greywacke with scatterings of rock and ash from more recent volcanic eruptions, these ranges are the oldest landforms in the park. To the south and east, around Lake Waikaremoana, the sedimentary rocks are

Above: Narrow channels and forest covered islands in Lake Waikareiti.

younger and softer, and the eroded sandstones, mudstones and siltstones have formed prominent scarps and long dipping slopes. Deep valleys such as the Aniwaniwa have been carved from softer mudstones, while more solid sandstones have formed ridges like the Panekiri Ridge. The whole landscape is thickly cloaked with forest, even on the 'tops' of ranges, and crystal clear lakes, rivers and streams are virtually all that break the green cover. This, combined with the region's high annual rainfall and frequent fogs and mists, give the park an ancient and primeval quality.

Lake Waikareiti, north of Lake Waikaremoana, is reached by a popular short walk from Aniwaniwa.

Lake Waikaremoana is the park's largest lake and central attraction, with thick forest tumbling to the water's edge and the dramatic Panekiri Bluff towering over its southern shores. The lake formed after a huge landslide 2,300 years ago blocked a narrow gorge along the Waikaretaheke River. Water backed up behind this natural dam to form a lake 248 metres deep. Hydro-electric development lowered the level by five metres in 1946, but despite this Waikaremoana retains its wild beauty and evokes a sense of eerie mystery; in Maori legend, this 'sea of rippling waters' is inhabited by a taniwha monster.

Te Urewera's thick native forest stretches across a variety of altitudes, and the vegetation pattern is always changing as a result of volcanic disturbances, fire and storm damage, and modification by possums and deer. At lower altitudes, the park's forests are dominated by rimu, northern rata, tawa and kamahi, but at higher levels beech trees take over with red and silver beech dominating, and mountain beech on well drained ridges. Even higher, silver beech assumes stunted forms and is festooned with mosses. The park experiences mild summers, but has a high annual rainfall (2,500–2,600 millimetres) and cool winters with frequent fog, high winds and snow, all of which combine with altitudinal variations to influence plant life. There are more than 650 species of plants in the park, many of them rare and vulnerable. A true rarity within the park is the only known individual of the plant 'X-it', which belongs to the Cunoniaceae family and has no known close relatives in New

Zealand. Nearby Whirinaki Forest, though not included in the park, is the finest example of the magnificent podocarp rainforests that once covered New Zealand's fertile lowlands, with tall dense stands of totara, rimu and miro.

Because of their large size and range of habitats, Te Urewera forests support a wide range of wildlife species, many of which are threatened. Rare North Island kokako can still be glimpsed here, and surveys indicate that the largest surviving kokako population may exist in the northern areas. Kaka, rifleman, North Island robin, weka, New Zealand falcon, ruru and yellow- and red-crowned parakeet are all commonly seen; at night North Island kiwi and morepork may be heard or chanced upon. There have also been recent unconfirmed sightings of bush wren and piopio, although these species are officially extinct. Blue ducks are found in a number of tributaries of the Rangitaiki, Waimana, Whakatane, Waioeka and Ruakituri Rivers, and Lake Waikaremoana. Long- and short-tailed bats are also found here – the forests are believed to be one of the last North Island strongholds for the more active short-tailed bat. A wide variety of invertebrates is present, and a population of the giant land snail *Powelliphanta marchanti* on the upper slopes of Manuoha is the northernmost occurrence of this genus. There are at least nine species of native fish, including the threatened koaro and kokopu, that inhabit the park's rivers and lakes.

Sand ripples in one of Lake Waikareiti's shallow bays.

Mature rimu and tawa forest is a feature of the vegetation near Te Puna hut on the Lake Waikaremoana Track.

The Tuhoe who originally settled and still live in the Urewera region, have long been an isolated people who have fiercely resisted some European influences (early this century their prophet Rua Kenana called his followers together at Maungapohatu in an attempt to create a Maori settlement independent of the western world). Te Urewera remains the centre of a largely traditional Maori way of life, especially for the Tuhoe people living in enclaves of Maori land within the park boundaries. Many of these enclaves are found on the shores of Lake Waikaremoana, which is revered by Tuhoe and other local iwi.

Old Maori trails through Te Urewera are the origins of many of its 600 kilometres of tracks. A wide range of short and day walks through luxuriant forest and past many waterfalls can be easily reached from Aniwaniwa. Lake Waikareiti, is an hour's walk from the Aniwaniwa Visitor Centre. One of the most popular and memorable tramping routes in the park is the 46 kilometre Lake Waikaremoana Track which follows the shores of the lake for most of its length. The track is a three to four day hike with huts and campsites along the way. Taking to the waters of Lake Waikaremoana by boat or kayak is another way to experience its many moods and its outstanding scenery of forest and cliffs. Picnicking, birdwatching, fishing, canoeing and boating are attractions for visitors in summer, and recreational fishing and hunting are both popular in spring and autumn.

North Island brown kiwi are more likely to be heard at night than seen. Because of its large size Te Urewera is an important sanctuary for North Island forest wildlife.

Aniwaniwa Falls, near the Aniwaniwa Visitor Centre.

Opposite: Lake Waikaremoana and the Urewera forest wilderness from high on Panekiri Bluff.

Mist hangs in beech forest on the Panekiri Range.

TE UREWERA NATIONAL PARK

Te Urewera National Park
Visitor Centre
Private Bag 2213
Wairoa
Phone: (06) 837 3803